ERINPHARM

Survival

by

John L. Fahey
2015

© ISBN 978-1-329-37816-2

Survival. Second Edition. Copyright 2015 by John L. Fahey. All rights reserved. Printed in the United States of America. No part of this book may be used or reproduced in any manner whatsoever without written permission except in the case of brief quotations embodied in critical reviews or articles. For information contact John L. Fahey, address at Erinpharm about_me page.

To dare to hope

To dare to hope, to dare to dream,
To think of things that might have been,
To wish upon a star, to want,
And will that things come true,
In dead of night to wait for dawn,
With hope, to bring a life to me, and you,
For if we bring ourselves to want enough,
In the light of day to keep the dream alive,
To nurture it, and give it life, to strive
To pass it on, to share it with the world,
To stand and look and see the sky that is and might
Once more again to dare to hope and dream.

© John L. Fahey 2011

Dedicated to all those who have been kind and helped me at
times of crisis, particularly my sister Patricia, and to the memory
of my mother, Aunt Josie, Aunt Maureen and Uncle Ken, and
last but not least my grandparents Thomas and Bridget Fahey.

This wondrous place

This wondrous place, this continent, this history
To which I came, a frightened boy, a hungering
For safety and for freedom from my fears,
Astonishing me with kindness and with help,
A people unlike those I'd known before,
Sunlight on open fields and an easing of my heart,
A place to lay to rest my hunger for relief,
A multitude of different ways of life,
The savory foods, the excitement and the cities,
The looking ahead to futures yet to come,
Opportunities and work no matter what my origins,
Come in, sit down, welcome to our homes,
That I could cry for easing of my heart and love of you,
A land to grow my crops and give myself to you,
My tears overflow for you America.

© John L. Fahey 2013

Chapter 1

After I was born a bastard, my father having vanished on hearing of my conception, George Orwell was writing Animal Farm just a few miles from Stockton-on-Tees. The terraced house I was born in was a short distance from the first passenger railroad station in the world. The midwife suggested my Christian names but it was well over seven months until my baptism, after my father was sought out, and found, in Manchester, and forced to marry my mother.

Such was my world in the year in which Animal Farm was written. I knew nothing of those things as I began to talk and learned to read just as I knew nothing of Aldous Huxley visiting more than a decade earlier the site of where I was later to start my working life in the Saxon town of Billingham where he described his awe of Imperial Chemical Industries as the stimulus to write Brave New World. Such is the innocence of a young lad struggling to make his way in the world unaware of the history around him.

It is perhaps appropriate then that my first post university job, several months of work before leaving England, was in the town of Berkhamstead, the place where the last possible Saxon King of England surrendered to William the Conqueror. In truth Edgar Atheling had been proclaimed as king by the Witan though never crowned. The last Saxon King Harold Godwinson had died in the battle of Hastings during that Norman invasion. So ended the Saxon monarchy of England; so ended my life in England.

My brother Tom used to say someone should write about our family in the sense meaning he, or I, or Terry. Not that he was excluding the collective our as in our Pat, and our Mary, our Josie and our Maureen, our aunt Nancy. There's enough to write about he'd say. We all lived through cataclysmic times. The great hunger of course long ago, and Thomas Wade and what he did, the world wars, the bravery and the shattered lives, crossing to England, the end of the second world war and then our arrival from one side of the Irish Sea to the other and back again.

Little did we know, when young, what the future would bring to our lives, unaware of our poverty, not looking ahead through those days of our minimal expectations, trying only to survive, looking for anything to ease the daily fears. We had no choice but to live through the years after that war, whole streets of brick rubble and burned timbers, ration cards, odd behaviors, strange attitudes, survivors knowing fear was over, the rain, and the cold, and being young, barely comprehending, beaten without reason, trying to survive, finding those things imprinting determination and resolve in me, adding to the other influences in my life, giving me a restlessness that has served me well.

Adversity can be the oddest thing. In some, when encountered young, it can provoke defiance. In the case of violent drunken households it stimulates the urge to survive, to run away, to seek another pathway. It is a two edged sword. For some it is eternal despair. For others it can be a jolt to intelligence and thinking, an opportunity to move on.

I was born at 21 Mill Street West in Stockton-on-Tees. It is an irony of the modern age that a photograph of that humble house exists today in the archives of Stockton Public Library so that at any time I can go online and look and see the house just before it was demolished, seeing in that picture the window at which my Saxon grandmother sat waiting for me, in the room where I learned to read, beside the alleyway where I played, below the room where I was born.

Ireland was neutral in that war. England was devastated; ration books for food, mourning and hunger for the working class. In the years after my Irish Grandmother Bridget would cross the Irish Sea with loaded bags of eggs, and butter, and chickens. My father would still beat his wife and children. The pubs at night were oases of war songs and defiance. Cod and chips were sixpence down the block. My English Grandmother Annie had a big glass battery for her radio, charging extra at the shop when needed. She was comfortable lighting a gas mantle flame in a fixture on the wall for light. She was frightened of the electric switch when the change came.

That winter I was almost five and I remember the dark and the light snow, walking down Leeds Street, seeing that terraced house and Grandma sitting in the front window by the light of a candle waiting for me to arrive from school to flip the electric

Survivor

switch. That was my first understanding of how some are slow to accept change.

That ground floor parlor room beside the alleyway is where my granny Annie Dobson finally welcomed in electric light, where from that alleyway I could see up a perpendicular street, Leeds Street, a few minutes walk, up to the top, from where to the left was, and is, Stockton Railway Station, that oldest and first passenger railway station in the world, from where later I fled north, across the border, into Scotland.

My life of course began earlier, born from an English mother Edna, with many sisters, Ivy and Vy, Annie, Jean and she called Edna May, Henry her father, in that working class terraced home, at the close of the war. My father had caused the pregnancy, and then he fled, leaving me in his denial, not being found, until by his parents, Tom and Bridget Fahey, coming from Ireland, appealed to by letter from my mother's parents, looked for him and brought him back when I was over seven months old. I am sure his parents were driven by the knowledge that their first grandchild, a boy, would have been incarcerated into a state home, and his mother another incarceration, under the laws of Ireland. For it was believed in Ireland at that time an unmarried mother carried with her a great sin, and the child was complicit in that sin. I was told in later years by my father's sister, my Aunt Josie, that the first marriage ceremony in a Registrar's Office was one in which my father had two black eyes and a split lip. My grandfather had been an honorable soldier in World War One. My father had the unenviable distinction of joining the British Navy and then being thrown out at the height of World War Two.

There was a later wedding in St. Mary's Church on Norton Road, after my Protestant mother had received instructions from the parish priest in her duties as a mother of a Catholic child. She kept her faith to the church though she never took the step of conversion. She was a good woman.

In my youngest years I became used to my father accusing my mother, and then battering her, shouting about her Norwegian boyfriend while he went missing, calling me a bastard, hitting me, hurting me, denying I was his son. But I never doubted that my father was indeed my father, and that was confirmed many decades later.

As a toddler I do remember some good times. The day when I asked my father what he was doing in the garden at the back of our council house in Primrose Hill, before Derby Street, and he told me he was planting lettuce and I in my innocence was puzzled at how he could be planting letters. The council house, one of many semi-detached brick houses on many streets built by the local council for the working classes at a modest rent, with a small front lawn and a back garden for growing vegetables, was a comfortable place with an upstairs and a downstairs, a flush toilet part of the house but separate in the sense that we would have to go out the kitchen door and go in the door to the immediate right, getting wet on cold windy nights.

There were the times he drilled me in the alphabet and had fun demonstrating to his pub friends late at night, reeking of beer and cigarettes, that I could recite, forwards and backwards, the alphabet, given any particular letter. He taught me how to tell the time. Then there was another time, when he flew into a rage, smashing windows and furniture, and I have a vivid memory when my mother took me and my sister Patricia by the hand, walking a mile in a thunderstorm on Mile House Road, in the dark, trees swaying overhead, us soaking wet and not caring because we were away from the havoc, seeking help from a policeman, frightened at returning, sleeping in fear that night, losing that house later because of his rages, because he would not stop.

A change came when I was six months beyond four years old. My mother took me to the local Catholic elementary school, St. Mary's school, on Norton Road. It was a long walk, crossing on a wooden bridge over railroad tracks. I was fascinated by the steam trains passing beneath. When we reached the school Sister Veronica took details from my mother while I explored. I stood on tiptoes and looked over the partition into the first grade class. I was repulsed. I saw kids playing with paints and plasticine clay, the unmistakable smell of shit. Then I crossed the hallway and peered into the second grade class. I underwent an epiphany. As I saw the alphabet displayed high on the wall around the room, from A to Z, I came to the startling realization that the order of the letters in a word gave its pronunciation. Up until then I had baffled myself trying to determine the meaning of the frequency of the letters in newspapers. It was profound and I do believe I learned to read that day.

Several days later I went missing from my school. I was found in the front parlor of Grandmother Annie Dobson's house nearing the end of an afternoon reading a book I had found; Grimm's Fairy Tales.

During the following winter I was taken to my grandparents' house in Roscommon, across the Irish Sea, a long train ride, and a ship, and another train ride, to freedom, in Ireland. My father had begun to resent me, and fear me. His anger at me had begun to grow. He had introduced terror to a child too young to understand the meaning of the word.

My grandparents lived in a two bedroom house, two floors, joined to an identical house each on about an acre of land, three miles from the town of Roscommon. My memories of that time and those precious several years are fragmentary but it was as if I had arrived in a magical land where the sky was brighter and the air smelled sweeter and everyone was kind and spoke softly and I was no longer you bastard; I had my own name, John. My grandfather, Thomas, had been given the house after marriage to Bridget Murray, for his service in World War One. He had built a chicken coop for dozens of chickens, a pig sty enclosure for several pigs, a tilled field for an endless supply of potatoes and cabbages, and a small covered building to keep the turf dry so my grandmother wouldn't have far to go from the back of the house to get turf for the fire.

I remember it as an idyllic existence. There was one large room with a huge walk in fireplace on the ground floor with a small back parlor room for special occasions, and stairs up to two bedrooms, one of them for me. It was a peaceful house, my grandmother cooking on the turf fire, oil lamps to light the rooms at night when my grandfather would come home from work. My heart expanded in love for my grandparents, inextricably mixed with the savory smell of slow cooked potatoes and cabbage, bacon sizzling in a cast iron pan, fresh baked bread with savory butter, as much milk as I could drink and the urgings of "eat John, eat so you can grow up to be a big lad". And of course fresh eggs for breakfast with more bread and butter and jam and roast chicken on weekends. After dinner we would kneel on the stone floor to say decades of the Rosary praying for the poor hungry children of the world: my grandfather knew of those children, he had been there.

Sometimes my grandfather's friends would visit late at night and they would sit around the turf fire with me on a little bench closest to the fire and they talked of Ireland's past and the days of resistance and rebellion. My grandfather would tell me, holding me enclosed in his arms, "John, you are the equal of any man be he the President of Ireland, or the King of England, or the captain of the Gaelic athletic team, but remember John the man who breaks stones by the side of the road and the woman who scrubs floors for a living is your equal too" He said that to me many times, impressing it on me, as if he knew we would have only a few short years together. It has been with me all my life and I have held it tight to my heart and soul.

And it was there I heard of Thomas Wade, my grandmother's grandfather, who had passed down honor for over a century, to his descendents. He had been one of the Catholic farmers in Connaught allowed to own his own land by the English. It had been in his family for generations and had a water wheel mill which ground grain into flour. He was a prosperous man by the values of the times and had many children. But the blight destroyed the potato crop and the English took all the other food out of Ireland and the people began to starve, year after year. An Gorta Mór it is called in the Irish language, the great hunger, and the years of that famine is expressed best in Irish since English does not properly express the cruelty and injustice of those years.

In the first year of the great hunger people were walking by the gates of the farm on the way another five miles to Roscommon town and after that forty eight miles to Galway and the coffin ships and sharks following the ships sailing to America for the dead bodies thrown overboard and hungry all the way. Thomas Wade set his wife and children baking bread and giving bread to all who passed their front gate. In the second year there were so many people there wasn't time to bake the bread so the hungry passers-by were each given a handful of flour. In the third year there were so many people flooding past the farm there wasn't time to grind enough grain into flour so they began to give a handful of grain, his wife and children standing throughout the day with sacks and barrels of grain by the gate. In the fourth year it was all gone and the land was devastated and Thomas Wade's family began to starve and die. Thomas Wade and his wife had established an honor that their descendents needs must never forget.

For the first couple of years of my awakening to kindness my life was with Grandma during the day, listening to Radio Eireann, reading through the local newspaper, the Roscommon Champion, puzzling at the sections written in Irish and wanting so much to understand them, reading of farming news and sports, then waiting at the front gate looking down to the turn in the road for my grandfather to come home. He always came home at the same time. When I would see him come into sight my heart would surge with joy and happiness and I would turn and call out to my grandmother watching me from the front window and she would laugh and tell me "go on then" and that would be my permission to open the gate and run down the road to my grandfather who would lift me on to his shoulders and carry me back to the house. He would always bring me a gift, an apple, or peanuts, or an orange. He would sit with me in the small field beside the house and explain to me the ways of the world, telling me of plants and animals and how to raise them and care for them, showing me that I should always eat the skin of the orange after the succulent flesh even though it be bitter because it was good for the health.

The time came when I was taken to visit the Dolans a couple of miles down the road, nearer to town, and met my new friend Seámus Dolan. It was a wonderful sunny day, opening up more of Ireland to me, walking past the house of the Hanleys next to the village pump, then down past the curve in the road where to the right the house of the Flanagan widow with her grown twin daughters lived and then a short way with the boreen road sloping downward where on the left we stood for a while and talked with my grandmother's triplet brother Jack at the gate of his house and he was told it was my day to meet the Dolans so that I could prepare for school. He explained to me that the side of the boreen road we lived on was called Ballybohan and the other side of the road where the Dolans had their farm house was called Ballybride. He told me there was no need of numbers for the houses because the postman knew where everyone lived.

There were fields to the sides of the road and cattle grazing and hedges and low stone walls and it was peaceful with no traffic for there would only be an occasional person on a bicycle or a horse drawn farm wagon to interrupt the tranquility. Seámus became my great friend. In the early morning he would appear after breakfast and we would take about a half dozen cows from a nearby field and slowly urge them down the boreen to the milking sheds at his parent's house. Slowly and taking our time because to hurry the cows full of milk would not be good so we would let them ramble and graze as we walked behind them giving them an occasional thwack with a stick at the top of the tail to keep them moving. We talked of many things as young boys do and imagined great wonders awaiting us in the world we would explore.

It was a happy time for me as I reached the age of seven and it was time for us to go to the Christian Brothers School on the outskirts of Roscommon town. It was a time when men had to come for a pig to be taken away so I could get my first shoes and clothes and books for school. I really needed the shoes for that because a few hundred yards past the Dolan's house the boreen road reached a two lane tarmac road, too rough for my feet. That road was a long walk to school with fields to the right and to the left a view across a wide marsh to Roscommon Castle, tall and immense and magnificent though in ruins, until we would reach houses and other buildings and the feeling we were actually in town.

I began to learn Irish and it baffled and enchanted me while arithmetic and mathematics drew me into a never ending exploration. By then I had become a voracious reader in the English language, reading anything I could get my hands on so needed no help for that, just needing newspapers and magazines and books and dictionaries and advertisements on packages. If we were poor I never knew it.

I was barely two years going to school with the Christian Brothers, happy with collecting eggs in the morning, going to the village pump to bring home a white enamel bucket of fresh water, helping drive slowly the cows down to the milking sheds on the way to school, learning the Irish language, always having clean clothes and a fresh bed to sleep in when bad news arrived in the form of my almost forgotten father. He was taking me back to England, taking me away from my security and my happiness. I was frightened of this strange man who looked at me as though his smile and face was always on the verge of turning into anger. I didn't know it was the last time I would see my grandfather. In not knowing I was not totally plunged in despair. I always had the hope I could come home again.

It was 1953. I was nine. I was back at St. Mary's Elementary School, still standing safe with its Church of the same name, behind tall brick walls, on a main road, Norton Road, beside the streets of bombed and burned houses, given separate classes in calligraphy for a while, joined with my peers, both boys and girls, studying for national examinations, the 11 plus, anonymous in that I'd be given a number, the papers scored in a remote place, so that the poor would not be identified, would be given a fair chance. It was a fact of life in those days, in England, that all children would be subjected to several days of what was commonly believed was intelligence testing when they would reach about the age of eleven and I had to prepare for that.

My return to England and the Catholic elementary school, surrounded by those streets of abandoned, bombed and burned brick row houses, reading books from the junior library down on Wellington Street gave me new ideas of the world. I was now in with my younger sister Patricia and baby Mary. We lived in a row house, 35 Derby Street, the worst part of town, with the other poor people. I learned quickly not to let my father see me reading. "I'll poke out your eyes with a red hot poker if I catch you reading again," he would threaten, pulling the poker from the coal fire, the tip cherry red, waving it at me and setting my heart thudding in my chest.

There were nights when he and my mother would come home from the pub in drunken revelry and life seemed almost normal as we were given little bags of potato crisps with a blue wrapped twist of salt. But it could turn violent with my mother crying and being attacked as she tried to put herself between him and me and my sisters. Going to bed with old coats to cover me I'd try to dream of Ballybohan and going back home, trying not to cry, hurting from the physical blows and torment of being again you bastard, him not believing I was his son.

A polio scare swept through the town with a sudden frightening alarm. Lines of mothers with children on the streets outside clinics, warnings, notices, then just as suddenly seeming to be over, became a foundation stone in my future. My friend Henry Chapman, sitting next to me in class, got polio, finished up in an iron lung, and I never saw him again. I was almost ten. The arrival of polio vaccination was as yet several years in the future. I was not conscious that I had escaped a terrible fate, did not realize until many years after that it was to be the first of many encounters with illness, with injury, with thoughts of fighting back against such a foe, determination hardening me against my fears.

Another chilling encounter with disease entered my life that year. Our beautiful sister Mary came down with scarlet fever and was taken into an isolation hospital on Mile House Road. We were told it was very contagious and Mary was going to die. Patricia and I borrowed bikes and pedaled north out of Derby Street, past the railway station, on up beyond Primrose Hill, to the forbidding grey stone hospital building. Mary was only just four years old. Patricia was eight. We knew we couldn't go in so we sat on our bikes on the side of the road and looked at the building. We were consumed with sadness that Mary was going to die and that our parents were not going to visit and we would not be let in. In my unshed tears I had a fierce determination that I would fight back against this, that somehow one day I would fight such a terrible disease. As it turned out Mary recovered and was back with us some months later. After that Patricia and I gave her special care and attention.

Survivor

Patricia and I had often been complimented on our good looks, with deep blue eyes and amber brown hair and fair complexion, thin from lack of enough food, being told by others that surely we would become movie stars but our Mary had a true beauty about her, a perfection so extraordinary that sometimes we'd persuade her to sit perfectly still when strangers would come to the house, pretending she was a doll. And Mary would go along with that joke, a gentle smile on her face, small as she was, until she would move and talk and cause merriment. She never did grow as tall as the rest of us but she always remained slim and beautiful.

Each day was a welcome oasis of safety in that school with a small bottle of milk in the morning and walking with teachers each day at noon a short distance away to a hall with long tables in rows and a kitchen steaming with savory dinners of meat and potatoes and cabbage, fish on Fridays, sweet desserts, and back to English, and arithmetic, and the beginnings of algebra, and geometry, on to simple trigonometry and an introduction to the labyrinth of logarithms.

At night I was at war with a man I feared was out to cause me serious harm. But I had allies. My mother Edna May took the brunt of his violence. At that time she had few choices. She was soon to bear another child, and there was me, and my younger sisters Patricia, and Mary. Dad's sister Josie and her family lived a couple of miles away and my mother's mother Annie Dobson and my mother's younger sister Aunt Jean lived together just a few streets away in my birth home on Mill Street West. At times my refuge from my beatings became Granny Dobson's house, precious evenings where I would feel safe. The house was quiet with the radio on low and the clock on the wall ticking, grandma knitting, Aunt Jean cooking dinner, and special times for me lying on the carpet to listen to radio episodes of the adventures of Dan Dare, an outer space series that enthralled me with the ideas of the solar system. I'd be given two pennies on Tuesday to go across the street to buy the Dandy comic, and then on Thursday another two pennies to buy the Beano, another comic. Sometimes on a Saturday I'd go with granny into the crowded market on the High Street, always hand in hand, and be given a toffee apple. Sunday afternoon was

11

the day of the week to cook a roast beef and the kitchen had to be cleared for Aunt Jean because she was an expert at making a crispy golden Yorkshire pudding to be served alongside the roast beef. She would garnish it with chopped lettuce and scallions in a little vinegar and it would make me feel loved and taken care of.

There would be other days on weekends when the house would be in a whirl of activity of cleaning and granny pounding clothes in a possing barrel filled with hot soapy water brought from the gas stove in the kitchen in large pans. That was done in the back yard with a long handled wooden posser while putting the wet clothes through a hand turned mangle to squeeze out the water so the clothes could be put on lines across the back yard to dry, the yard door open to the alleyway for the breezes to help dry the washing, the smell of the soapy water filling the air with a delightful fragrance. There were some times when my drunken father would turn up in the alleyway from a nearby pub and there would be shouting and protesting and angers about me while I would run inside and hide, shaking and in fear again. But he would not be allowed in and I'd have a respite until returning to Derby Street later that night, to havoc after the pubs closed, to being a bastard again, to curses, and kicks and blows, and sleep, lying atop my Gaelic grammar books, trying to dream of Ballybohan and escape.

I became an altar server at the church and was comforted by the serenity and solemnity of early morning Mass. I learned the Latin responses and was awed by the sonorous phrases, feeling I was part of another existence, distant from my daily life. I liked to serve at the first Mass at six o'clock. It was a special magic to get up before dawn and walk beneath streetlights and stars wrapped against the cold, recovering from the night before.

It was a scramble surviving until that March in which I became 11 and had to get a bus out to a northern part of town where a modern brick Protestant school had given its students a week off so that the school would be a testing center. So for three days, morning and afternoon, I took the tests, taking the bus back each night, just going from day to day knowing I'd have to put up with an inevitable series of punches and kicks and blows of one sort or another when I returned home. I just had to keep my distance and I was quick though just not quick enough sometimes. Often enough late night drunken rages would erupt into violence and screaming and crying and us kids out on the street. It seemed to be an inevitable sort of life, a life to be negotiated with pathways of avoidance and running and fear.

I feel there is a special sort of daily apprehension for children as young as we were in that kind of environment. For me, as I am sure it was for my sister Patricia, seventeen months younger, it was a long series of good days and bad days interspersed with violent drunken rages of our father and attempts by other people to bring some comfort to our lives. The streets at night brought a threatening sort of freedom, away from the violence of our father, alone and often cold, with a fear of attack from local kids our age that had their own lives to survive. We were used to the fact that we would not get birthday presents or Christmas presents and Patricia and I would sometimes fantasize what it would be like to be in the orphanage on Buckingham Road, hearing the laughter of children at play behind the tall brick wall. They, we knew, got presents at birthday and Christmas times. There was one time when my father's sister Maureen and her soon to be English husband Ken came by on Christmas Eve bearing gifts, pen and pencil sets, handkerchiefs, toys for Mary and the baby Thomas, and attempts at normalcy. Our father flew into a drunken rage, throwing the presents on the coal fire, putting one boot on the presents to make sure they burned, as he warded off attempts to stop him by Maureen and Ken and my mother. It is still a vivid memory to me of fleeing to the back alley behind the house consoling Mary, her crying and Patricia and I saying over and over again "don't cry, when we grow up we'll get you presents, ourselves, me and Pat."

My father was both violent and strong. Few could resist him. I was just eleven and Pat was almost ten. We could only depend on each other. When I passed the 11 plus, the only boy in my class at St. Mary's elementary to do so, I gained entry to further education at a grammar school, St. Mary's College in Middlesbrough, about five miles away, which I could only get to by bus, from Stockton High Street. The college was run and administered by Marist priests

Survivor

and had its own church on the grounds. To my surprise it brought a respite from being you bastard, not that my father was proud of me, but that entry had gained my parents an education grant, more beers for my father, more struggling for my mother.

In the week before my first classes my mother bought me a navy blue blazer, the proper uniform being too expensive, and stitched the school badge on the pocket and then an hour before that first bus ride took me into town to buy my required protractor set and gym shorts and shoes, bought from her wages. My mother by that time was working early morning hours cleaning floors in a nearby cinema, the Empire Cinema, and was able to make sure I would get the bus on time. I know she was proud of me. In later years I reflected often on the fact that my mother, though not Catholic, married to my father who avoided the Church and the priests, nonetheless made sure we all went to Catholic school, first communion, confirmation, and to Mass every Sunday and Saints day. There must surely be a special place in Heaven for a mother like that.

Emboldened by the temporary truce with my father I took advantage of his drunken good humor one day and persuaded him that I could get a job delivering newspapers if I had a bike and I could pay for it with installments. To my amazement his mood lasted long enough to get him into Curry's bicycle shop in town, on the High Street just across from the town hall, and within hours I was riding my new ten speed bike to the newsagent's shop where I had been promised the job of delivering morning and evening newspapers from Monday to Saturday. So began my first regular income. I didn't care that my father would hit me if I didn't give him my paper money. I had gained another step toward freedom, a glorious feeling of power as I would finish my morning delivery and cycle toward school. I had chosen a Raleigh bike, a racing bike, with dropped handlebars and ten derailleur gears, blue with white striping, and a large saddlebag fastened to the rear of the seat. It was my pride and joy and it was gloriously mine and I learned to keep it in racing shape, oiling and cleaning the gears, repacking the ball bearings in the wheel hubs, tightening wheel spokes, keeping the tires at a proper hard inflation pressure, having a bicycle lock

Survivor

and chain for whenever I had to keep it safe. I was paid ten shillings once a week.

On some market days Pat and I would go to the outdoor market in town and use some of my money to buy 'broken biscuits', sugar cookies sold in loose bags, and bruised fruit, apples and pears, and take Mary and little Thomas and have an orgy of eating on the benches in the Protestant graveyard at the end of the High Street. I knew that when we went home my father would demand my paper money, and hit me, and become enraged when he would go through my pockets and find less than he expected. I didn't care. I was defiant. It was as if all four of us together had won, had gained a victory. Looking back now I wish I had done it more often but then it is quite possible my father would have hurt me more than I could have recovered from. My job gave me a new determination in life, to pay a weekly installment on my bike at the Curry's bicycle shop on the High Street on time, so I could keep my bike, not have it taken away from me, doing it before going back to Derby Street, learning resolve and the inevitability of facing my father's anger, feeling safety in my hidden little payment book.

Around about that time my mother got me another job, babysitting two nights a week, for a young couple with three very young girls. Their name was Mr. and Mrs. Arthur Roe and they were of higher class than us, living on the upper floor of a building on Bishopton Lane, a thoroughfare of shops, within a short walk of Derby Street. Mr. Roe owned the lower floor of the building which was a wallpaper store owned by his family and there were aspects of wealth throughout that large second floor of many rooms. There was a telephone and a television. The television amazed me and I soon got over my fear of switching it on and off and watching the shows in black and white. The telephone I wouldn't touch, even when it rang, for it was too much out of my personal experience to know what to do if I lifted the receiver. It was to be a place safe away from my father after I finished my paper route; it was a place to do my homework. The little girls would be in bed, all I had to do was sit and watch television and wait for them to come back home, to collect my two shillings, to leave the safety for that evening.

15

Survivor

I have one very distinct memory from my first week at St. Mary's College. It was at my first Gym class where we were all assembled on a stage overlooking the exercise floor and told to change to our gym clothes, shorts, singlet and shoes. My mother had made sure I had the apparel but as I stood there on that stage and began to change I had to retreat into a corner, trying to hide, embarrassment and shame enveloping me, unshed tears overwhelming me, finding that other boys had clothing beneath their short pants, clothing I was to find out was called underpants. That day was an agony for me but I didn't cry until I was alone later that day. In the early evening I shared my shame with my sister Pat and told her I had seen the underpants I needed in Woolworths but I didn't know how to buy them. We pooled the few coins we had together and went into town to the Woolworths and while I, frightened and in shame, stood outside, my ten year old sister Pat went into that store and bought my first two pairs of underpants. Then we ran home as though it was a great adventure. All boys should have a sister like that.

Going to St. Mary's gave me a guaranteed meal every day Monday through Friday with a small bottle of milk mid morning. At other times all of us had to look for other sources of food, depending on the sympathy of others, Granny Dobson, Aunt Josie, cleaning women co-workers with my mother, for food in Derby Street was sporadic and uncertain in coming, my father yelling that during the war people were lucky to get an egg a week. But none of us ever stole food, or begged for it, we were used to relying on school lunches, going without, getting chips from the fish and chip store, going to bed hungry, being resilient, making do with apples or knowing how to turn up at a friend's house just before dinnertime, just not the same house too often. From my first days at the school I would help the staff in the dining hall clean up the tables and stack the chairs after the lunch hour and I would get extra desserts and more on my plate every day from the women serving the food. It wasn't until many years later that I realized those kind ladies were seeing the bruises and abrasions and worn clothes that I unconsciously carried with me throughout my school days.

I began to go straight to the quiet of the church after stacking the chairs and for the rest of the lunch hour I would pray at a Station of the Cross, imploring God to release me from my agony, begging for relief in my prayers, asking that God sent a wayward bus to take out my father so that me and my sisters and brothers could go live in the orphanage. It never occurred to me that my mother would still be there for us, imbued as I was by the times and my mother, a battered wife, a shadow trailing my father.

Derby Street was a cul-de-sac street of terraced brick houses, slate roofs, concrete and curb beneath the ground floor windows and wooden doors, cobblestones separating seven houses on one side facing an equal number on the other, with a tall brick wall at the end of the street with a tiny garden on each side for the houses up against the wall. At the opening of the street to the outside world there was a narrow alleyway that served as a back lane behind the houses that fronted onto the main street, Wellington Street. The alleyway ran in both directions with other cul-de-sac streets parallel to Derby Street and somehow to my young perceptions the houses that fronted onto Wellington Street were inhabited by a better class of people, not poor like us, not people we could ever even know. On the other side of Wellington Street our street, Derby Street, like the other cul-de-sac streets, continued outward with many more terraced houses on each side, intersecting with Mill Street West where I was born, and then further outward toward Stockton Railway Station and much grander houses and larger houses with bay windows.

Without us even being told we knew we were among the poorest of the poor, with grass sprouting among the cobblestones and divisions even among the families living next to each other, not talking to each other, barely even glancing at us or acknowledging we existed when chance encounters would bring us within eyesight of each other. There were two other families on that street we recognized as being at our level; one family with sons older than us who were violent and criminal, another with kids about our age, even poorer than us and even more ignorant, so we had someone to look down on and pity. Beyond the brick wall there were similar rows of streets, terrace upon terrace, a grid of working class homes,

Survivor

striving hard working people intermingled with those who battered their families and worse, clean colorful curtains at windows and bright freshly painted doors marking families doing their best, tattered dirty curtains and even old bed sheets, marked and dirty front doors letting others know of the family living inside, advertising despair and anguish.

Wellington Street to the left ended at the Co-operative storage sheds defining the railway tracks, on the right leading down into the main street of the town, called the High Street. It was a street indelibly inscribed in my memories, holding with it so many instances and fears and hopes. A short distance down Wellington Street was Stockton main library with a junior library across from it and beyond that were shops lining the sides of the street. In those days there were separate shops for butchers and greengrocers and breads and cakes, with a small Co-op store next to the junior library, for canned goods and the many other foods and household needs such as candles and matches and salt and flour and eggs. My Aunt Jean worked there. Bacon would be bought at the butchers. We were never bought cakes and were used to 'day-old' bread. We didn't know any different. After all we knew our place in life. These better things on display were for the people who lived in the grander houses, not us. At several points on the street were buildings we knew to be Protestant churches. We ignored those; they had little relevance to what we were comfortable with. After the shops, just before reaching the High Street, were the multi storey Co-op stores selling all kinds of goods from clothes to furniture, gargantuan compared to the individual shops on each side and facing them. The Co-op stores gave a bank book to each customer and purchases were recorded with receipts so that each couple of months a dividend based on total purchases was placed in the bank book. I thought it was the grandest thing. On reaching the High Street, the widest street in England we were told, there was a market day every Wednesday and Saturday, covered temporary stalls selling everything imaginable, a long double mile that had been in existence since Saxon times, anchored at one point by the Town Hall with an imposing clock tower, at another by the 'Shambles', a brick building with vendors selling fresh slaughtered meat and locally caught fish and shellfish, and yet a third point in between with the town's public toilets, brick and glazed glass buried into the ground, walking down steps, kept tiled and clean and busy. On market days the town was crowded, the pubs full, fish and chip shops with long lines, double-decker buses slowly driving through traffic and throngs of shoppers, the High Street filled with people from miles away and from other smaller towns in the region, alongside the river Tees.

I had been fortunate in my years living in Ireland; living close to cows and chickens and pigs, gaining immunities, exploring fields and streams, protection all around me. Those few years had been idyllic. I had memories of my grandparents and Thomas Wade and Nancy Fahey and the Irish language that I was able to take with me back to England. It helped me survive my new daily life in Stockton. I had my Irish grammar books hidden from my father and I never lost my dreams of a better life ahead, of reading on to find the clue on how to escape to safety.

The librarian in the junior library took me across the street to the main library on Wellington Street and persuaded them that I should be given an adult library card even though I was only eleven. I remember her saying that I had read everything in the junior library several times and I should be given an exception despite my age. It became an epiphany and it fueled my drive to escape. I was allowed to take out two fiction and two non-fiction books every day. I took full advantage of that. I would choose fiction books at random by the titles and after perusing a few pages. Those books I consumed, reading with fervor akin to an insatiable hunger. The non-fiction I took a totally different approach. I decided to start at A and work my way through to Z, not really reading the book unless I could understand some of it but nonetheless turning each page and glancing at it for a second before moving on. I had a deep set conviction that one day I would turn a page and the solution to my fears would leap out at me and I would be able to suddenly move myself into a much better life. It was complicated hiding books from my father and finding places to read where my father could not catch me but I managed. There were many places in parks and cemeteries where I found special secluded spots to read and on rainy days the library had a reading room inhabited by old men smoking and reading newspapers. I never felt shy about reading there and in an obscure way I felt that those old men would protect me if my father would burst in looking for me.

Our Aunt Nancy of course I never got to know beyond memory of her. But then the story of her life burned strongly in me, with imaginings of her as a little girl in our house in Ballybohan, the turf fire warming the room, her father, my grandfather, talking of his father and the years of An Gorta Mór, the great hunger, her mother talking of the awesome deeds of Thomas Wade, and why we should all follow in his path, why his life placed an obligation on following generations, in honor and in respect. We were told of how she became a nurse aircraftwoman first class and left Ireland to volunteer in the British air force and to tend tuberculosis patients in a military hospital in Wales, knowing she could get the disease, and she did, returning home to Ballybohan, to die in the arms of her father, passing the illness to him. Grandma Bridget could never utter the actual words, saying to me years later in the soft cadence of Connaught, looking up at the photograph of her on the wall of the parlor, "she went to England and she got the cold and she came home and she died". In that way Nancy joined the history of the family; giving her young life in the cause of compassion. She did receive a memorial gravestone from the English, in the graveyard in Roscommon. It's been replaced now with a family headstone, as the years have gone by.

To be born poor in those days in England, and for that matter anywhere in the British Isles, brought with it a particular kind of ineradicable oppression in that the event of birth was on land that had been owned, possessed, occupied, and defined as belonging to the upper classes of society. That I, and my sisters and brothers, survived those years and accomplished more than anyone could possibly have expected is a monument to our relatives who were there for us during the times of our greatest crises.

Going to St. Mary's College each school day, Monday through Friday, after my paper round, involved getting out of the house fast, after a quick clean-up, a cup of tea, some buttered toasted bread from under the gas stove grill, then walking out of

Survivor

Derby Street down Wellington Street to the High Street and then a long walk to the far end where a bus for St. Mary's students would be waiting. If I missed the bus and had to take a council double-decker it would drop me off a few streets from the school. And often sometimes, on days it did not rain, I'd just go straight from my early morning paper route, missing breakfast, and cycle straight to school. I'd keep my books and homework in the large saddlebag I kept attached to the back of the seat, since in some mysterious way my father left my bike and saddlebag alone, though if I left my books out he'd throw them on the fire.

My mind was continually in a ferment of thoughts of survival and escape, the days going by with ideas and plans, always comforted with my memories of Ballybohan and the knowledge of fields and slow cooked bacon and potatoes on the turf fire, as real to my memory and my tears as the streets I walked or cycled from one place to another. I'd think often of the hundreds of my cousins who had never been born, told of them by my grandfather, telling of the famine days and the great hunger, children dying while still babies, few surviving, going back to his parents and grandparents time, and so much anguish and sorrow, so few left to tell of cousins lost. Surely I thought to myself that if the hunger had not happened then I'd have protection belonging to a great tribe of uncles and aunts and cousins, resisting my father's angers, holding me tight in the soft cadences of Roscommon, keeping me safe with tales of Gaelic courage in the face of adversity.

In my defiance I did not allow my father to see me cry when he beat me and shouted at me, cursing at me, hurting me. I would hold in the pain, letting the tears come when I was alone late at night, lying beneath the old coats, making a commitment to faith that I would never let a curse word or obscenity pass from my mouth. At times even the healing power of tears from my eyes became lost to me, my anguish becoming submerged in the ache of dry eyes, in my resolve not to let my father win his war against me. That gave me strength. In later years that was commented on by others, that I would not cry, could not cry, for myself, no matter what the circumstances, but that the tears would flow readily when seeing the suffering of others. So I do know of the healing powers of tears and welcome them when they come, for in this troubled world I often see of children in other places suffering from the angers and cruelties of adults in ways even worse than we had to endure, even not surviving. In that sense when I read in newspapers or see on television horrible things happening to children like we were I let the tears flow from my eyes easily and readily while I attempt to draw some small comfort from the knowledge that there is an innocence in the young coming from a lack of knowing that the cruelty and impoverishment of their daily lives is unfair, undeserved, and not their fault. I want so much to let those children know that it will not be unending if they strive to survive. I want to tell them to keep reading, to keep learning, to keep a hold on hope.

My sister Patricia, after she escaped and married, devoted her whole life and work to such children. She has helped to guide thousands. She became a family court judge who puts abusive fathers into jail. If these words of mine can encourage such children to seek out those who will help them escape, those who will be kind, those who will give good direction, those like my sister Patricia, then my account will serve a good purpose. Those children should know that there are some adults who will care and will be kind, and that the compassion will be genuine. I found that to be so in my life and this account will honor each of the people I found, like milestones pointing the way ahead, giving me a helping hand at times of crisis, letting me know of human kindness.

For Patricia, and Mary, and Thomas, and Terrence who was born when I was past eleven, we lived in such a life of innocence. We lived from day to day in that slum house on Derby Street, not having the perceptions that would come to us later in life, in later years wondering and marveling that we still lived, remembering bringing each of us in our own way to caring for others, doing honor in our life to the memory of Thomas Wade and Aunt Nancy.

Most evenings before the pubs closed at half past ten were a special time for Patricia and me, several hours left alone. Mary was a beautiful and very quiet little girl, smiling all the time. Thomas by this time was almost a year old. It seemed quite normal to me that when Thomas needed his nappy changing it was up to me to change him, washing off the shit from the fabric in the kitchen sink, the

Survivor

cold water cascading through my hands while Patricia cleaned and powdered his bottom so we could put on a fresh nappy. The gas supply for the gas stove, and the electricity for the lights, was regulated by a meter in a small low room behind a wooden door in the living room. If the electricity went off or the gas stove didn't light then it was my task to open that door and go in with lit candle or small flashlight (we called that a torch) to put a coin in a slot and turn the dial to hear it drop. I detested that task. When I'd open the door to my light cockroaches would scatter under my feet and I'd move as fast as possible, shuddering as they would crunch beneath my shoes. Black beetles we called them and I've had a horror of them all my life. The house we lived in, a terraced house of brick with a slate roof, two rooms up and two down, with a kitchen at the back and a small back yard enclosed with a brick wall about six feet tall, was all we had. It was a rented house and we were continually weeks behind on the rent, my mother desperately cobbling the money together each week, us kids warned to hide inside and be quiet when the rent collector would come banging on the front door. I dreaded those times, frightened that we would be thrown out on the street, and learned then that rent must always be paid, and paid on time down at the rent office on the High Street to avoid the banging on the door.

The living room window looked out on a yard which had a flush toilet under its own slate roof, brick walls with a small window, set next to another identical space for the coal that was delivered from the alleyway behind. There was a door to the alleyway, the ground was concrete, and a small grate under the kitchen window allowed rain run-off to drain away. The walls of the toilet were whitewashed and there was a nail in the wall to hold squares of torn up newspaper for us to wipe our bums. It was often fetid and would become blocked up and someone would have to use a long wire opened from a coat hanger to poke the clogged shit and newsprint free. One year the small window in the wall became broken and it was left that way after, the winds and breezes whistling in, clearing the air of the stench. At the top of the stairs in the house, with a bedroom on each side, was placed a metal bucket for piss and shit at night. Incongruously my mother at some time had obtained a large print of the Last Supper in a frame and she had mounted it high on the wall above the bucket. My mother was really trying her best to bring some hope into our lives, overwhelmed by our surroundings, never missing a morning cleaning other people's dirt from cinema floors, bringing home the money for food for us and beer for my father, putting her Protestant faith in the hands of the Catholic priests.

About the time my parents got the education grant for me to go to St. Mary's College my mother was able to persuade my father the kitchen needed hot water for us to wash our faces. Up until then all we had was cold water from a tap over the kitchen sink. For a cleaning of the body before that we had to boil water in large pans on the gas stove and pour that into the sink, a rubber stopper in the drain hole. It was a cursory affair, done rapidly at quiet times and not often, the door to the living room temporarily closed with Patricia on the other side watching out for me, that I would not be interrupted. The day came when an instant hot water device was mounted next to the kitchen window and it became a delight to switch it on and watch the gas flames heat the slow stream of water coming from the spout at the bottom of the white enamel cylinder. It was as if a normalcy had entered our lives but the kitchen was still grimy and had dirt in crevices and black beetles hiding in the walls and beneath the stove, scattering at night when the light was switched-on as we would go out through the kitchen door to the toilet.

We had several years earlier acquired a black and white mongrel dog we called Spot and she gave us unceasing love, sleeping in an alcove in the living room atop old coats that had become too ragged to use as coverings on our beds. One time Spot became pregnant and Patricia and I watched her give birth to six pups and even our mother's face relaxed and softened as she showed us how to make Spot comfortable and take care of her pups. For a couple of weeks the joy of seeing the puppies nuzzling up to Spot was as though watching that bonding was a compensation for the family comfort denied us. Then a day came of such incredible cruelty that it burned a scar in my heart that would never heal. My father made me watch as he put the puppies two at a time in a nylon sock and lowered it into the drain in the back yard; the metal grate lifted and shifted to one side, the puppies struggling as they drowned. That night in bed I wept and prayed to God in thanks that my father had not made my sisters and brother watch.

At night after my father and mother went out to the pub, it would be the job of Patricia and me to clean out the ashes from the fireplace grate and set that night's fire. Crumpled up newspaper first, then a criss-cross layer of a few wooden sticks bought in a bundle from a nearby store, then lumps of coal, the newspaper lit with a match and coaxed into burning by lying on the floor and blowing on the embers. I'd add more coal as the fire grew so that the room would warm against the chill of the night, would be warm for when our parents would return home, so I would not be punished for a cold house. I've enjoyed the ritual of making a fire ever since, the accomplishment warming my emotions as well as my body. Then Patricia and I would have a couple of hours of real pleasure because we had a large radio on a shelf above Spot's bed in the alcove and we'd take turns with the dial looking for music for us to dance around the room as though in doing so we could make the whole world a better place. Our favorite station was Radio Luxembourg, coming from Europe over the North Sea, hissing and crackling at times but us not caring about that at all, joyous at the easing of fear from our lives. Sometimes I would slowly turn the tuning knob and pick up Morse code from the ships in the North Sea and sometimes the crackle of men's voices calling from ship to shore. It would excite my imagination and I would add it to times of looking at the stars in the sky on a clear winter's night, knowing there were wonders for me to find, that all I had to do was keep looking to find a way to escape. And so there in that place, at that age, I began to develop my love of foreign places and music and dancing and astronomy.

This account is a story of a series of adversities I encountered and the ways in which I resisted despair for in truth if I had known then what was up ahead for me I could well have fallen into a darkness that would have taken the spirit from me. There were great trials ahead for me, problems and impossibilities I would have to learn to live with, parts of myself I could not heal, the intolerances

Survivor

of others I would have to endure. But memories of Ballybohan and the solemn serenity of my Catholic faith kept me alive, helped me always look ahead for better days, made me be strong for my sisters and brothers, and nurtured my incoherent longing for love and understanding. All these things brought me to a place in my heart that was ready to learn of compassion and were fertile ground for decades of learning how to care for others.

I was always hungry and that gave me the capacity to enjoy and appreciate any food that was available. The school lunches at St. Mary's College were to me a high point of my day, delicious and savory, my plate always wiped clean. I would demolish cabbage and potatoes as readily as meat, not discriminating between meat and vegetables, unknowingly developing a healthy nutrition pattern, not realizing my hunger was building my growth the right way. It would puzzle me that some of my classmates would have food preferences, not liking this thing or that, while they in turn would tease me for my appetite even to the point of wanting a full jug of water for myself while the other seven students at my table would make do with one. At home beans on buttered toast was as welcome as bags of chips from the nearby fish and chip shop, hot golden wedges of potato, sprinkled with salt and vinegar, with added 'scraps' of pieces of crispy batter fallen off the battered fish while frying in the deep vats of boiling lard. We would have to ask for scraps to be added to the bag of chips but the chips were only two pennies and the scraps were free. Sometimes we would get some fried cod to share when my mother would be able to cajole my father into a good mood so that we, as well as he, could enjoy the succulent taste of the flakes of cod. I've liked that fish all my life since.

At other times it seemed as if our fortunes were rising when bacon and eggs were placed on the table or my father cooked a stew of boiled cabbage and potatoes with chunks of salty mutton that filled me easily. Broken biscuits and bruised fruit from the market were a special treat. There were few foods I was reluctant to try. One food that only my father liked became the focus of a memory. He liked mushrooms cooked in butter. I knew that and so one day when I was reading and doing my homework on a bench in a secluded section of a cemetery that was several miles from our house I developed a daring plan. I'd seen a lot of mushrooms growing on a pile of turned sod beneath trees where recent graves hadn't yet received headstones. I thought in my mind that surely mushrooms growing on graves must be poisonous. So I picked a great bag of them and took them home. I watched my father cook them in sizzling butter and eat them with great relish and was in a fever of anticipation throughout the hours he was gone at the pub, disappointed when he arrived home drunk and violently shouting as usual, demanding of me that I sing the rebel song Kevin Barry for him, in good humor with me, a semblance of fatherhood, danger in the room with me. That night I slept lightly thinking maybe the poison would work slowly but my attempt at patricide was a failure. I never again thought of doing him in, retreating instead to my entreaties to God, praying in the church.

Another memory of that room involved our Aunt Josie, his sister, who one night was brought to the house during a several hour long drunken rampage. She was protecting my mother who was trying to make peace by cooking rashers of streaky bacon in a cast iron pan on the gas stove. It reached the point where my father had me cornered, unable to escape, crunched in a corner with my arms over my head, enduring his shouts and kicks and blows, when Josie, god bless her, came out of the kitchen with the heavy frying pan handle grasped in her two hands and flung the hot bacon grease and sizzling bacon at him and as he screamed and went to attack her she raised the pan high above her head and with full force brought it down on my father's head. He fell to the floor with blood pouring from his head but nonetheless continued his drunken rant and attempted to get up but before he could lever himself off his elbows Josie lifted the pan again and with a furious force hit him again. He didn't get back up and the air was filled with frightened crying and comforting. He was in bed for three days after that and we had a sort of truce and I'd gained a great love and admiration for my Aunt Josie. It seemed as though that had subdued him for several weeks but he was back to his usual ways soon enough.

There were times on returning from the pub in a good humor my father would talk of going to live in Australia. At that time

Survivor

people in Britain could apply at Australia House in London to migrate to Australia and it would only cost ten pounds each parent and children free, being taken by ship, with food and entertainment for many weeks, arriving to be given a job on arrival. It would be a one way trip with no return. I'd eagerly agree with my father, encouraging him, wanting it to happen, for I'd read in a newspaper that the pubs in Australia closed at six in the evening and I thought that would help my father keep a good job and most definitely my hard working mother would get a better job than cleaning other peoples' dirt from cinema floors. Though I kept secret my knowledge about the pubs closing early in the evening it never came to pass, no matter how often I encouraged his drunken talk. It was said by other men in later years that my father could turn his hand to many kinds of labor and could have made something of himself if he wasn't always drunk.

The other Irishmen from the pub he would drink with were of varying sorts of character. Some, like him, had a pattern to their lives, working the required six months to earn benefits then claiming illness to get a 'doctors note' from a compliant physician so that they could get six months of 'dole', the weekly unemployment payment, until that would run out and they would have to get work again. My father's illness, he claimed, was bronchitis and he could develop a most convincing racking cough spitting up gobbets of phlegm when the time to go get the dole would arrive. In that respect the drunkenness and constant smoking of Woodbine cigarettes along with the coal and wood smoke of our environment helped make his stratagem work for him. So at least in one way or another he always had money coming in even though much of it went to the publicans and tobacconists and the weekend betting on horse races and football matches, that money going to a man in an alley just off Mill Street West, furtive because it was not legal betting that way. My mother's wages from cleaning other people's dirt from cinema floors, the 'child allowance' paid from the government for each child beyond the first, and my education grant supplemented the family income so that we were not paupers and had shoes and clothes.

28

Survivor

During times of collecting the 'dole' my father did all sorts of jobs and often would take me with him to help. There was a time when I was taken to a bungalow in a respectable part of the town where two old ladies lived. They had hired my father to repair a concrete pathway along the side of the bungalow that led from a small front lawn to a back garden overgrown with weeds. In the process of repairing the pathway he taught me how to 'float' concrete, kneeling on a board across the slurry, smoothing the newly laid path. The old ladies made a deal with my father, that he clear the back garden of weeds and he dig it over to plant vegetables for himself and keep it tidy. There was a stone patio at the back of the bungalow with another small lawn separating it from the soon to be tilled and planted garden, only a small area and nothing like the field my grandfather had in Ballybohan but I was overjoyed to have cabbage and potatoes growing in my life again. We uncovered a cold frame where my father planted lettuce seed and at the back of the garden I found a vigorous rhubarb patch, a plant I was totally unfamiliar with but soon learned to enjoy breaking off a stalk and washing it, cutting off the end to expose the tart green flesh with the ruby red skin running up to the large thick heavily savoyed green leaf. Dipping the cut end in sugar to counter the tart taste and biting off a chunk became another taste in my life, another food to take home to my sisters and brothers. The old ladies arranged with my father for me to mow their two small lawns each week with a push mower kept in a small shed attached to the side of the bungalow. My task was to mow the lawns, trim the edges with hand shears, then clean and oil the mower afterward. I liked the feeling of working to make a good job of the task, taking pride in the tidiness of my accomplishment, liking the praise I got with a glass of limeade and a shilling. Within weeks another old lady a short distance away hired me to mow her small front and back lawn for yet another shilling. So now I was soon to be twelve and I already had three sources of income with the lawns, my baby sitting job, and my regular morning and evening newspaper route. In a strange way that led to an easing of demands from my father to give him my earnings. Perhaps he had grown weary of running after me and hitting me to get my money, finding that usually I'd managed

Survivor

to pay for my bike installment and fish and chips and comics and bus fares before he'd catch me and go through my pockets. So a tacit understanding seemed to come into being where I paid my own way and he ended his attacks for money, though I made sure my pockets were usually empty when he would come home from the pub. In that way I learned responsibility and reliability and the determination to pay my own way. They were valuable lessons for the years I had ahead.

Survivor

Chapter 2

In those early years at St. Mary's College my life settled into a regular routine with my fears and hopes nurtured with my hunger for knowledge. I gained encouragement from the kindness of others. My father's sister Maureen had come to Stockton and got a job as a bus conductress on a double-decker bus, wearing a uniform and having a ticket dispenser at her belt. Sometimes when I missed the bus to school it would happen that the double-decker I'd get would have Maureen on board with her boyfriend Ken Easby driving the bus. Ken was an Englishman from a respectable working class family on Hind Street, a sort of superior area of row houses near a public Park, Ropner Park. Ken was a short fellow with a ready laugh and kindness in his voice but in being English wasn't much liked by my father. He was going to night school taking classes in engineering. He would always turn and wave to me with encouraging words as I'd get on the bus and as I'd get off at my destination. It would make me feel special and proud, giving me the urge to stand straight and upright.

The day came when Maureen and Ken were to get married. I was chosen to be a page boy with my sister Patricia a page girl. The reception after the wedding was held in Ken's parents' house on Hind Street. It became the occasion of an overwhelming memory for me that even to this day is vivid in my mind. I'd gone outside the house to play and was looking with great curiosity at a car with three wheels, unusual in appearance, when Ken appeared behind me and began explaining to me the features of the car. When he was done he settled back on his heels so that his head was on the same level as mine and he took hold of my shoulders with his hands and looked into my eyes. "John", he said, "your old man's a bastard, he's no good. I know what's going on. Keep studying at school and you'll get away. You come see us whenever you can." The words and sincerity of purpose burned brightly in the air around us. I felt the intensity of him trying to communicate with me and in that instant I came to realize that not all adult men were a

31

danger to me. He became a man I could trust and be comfortable in his presence. I often wished he was my father.

After the wedding Ken and Maureen got a caravan to live in just off the side of the road in a small field about eight miles away in the small hamlet of Urlay Nook, close to Eaglescliffe, near Yarm-on-Tees, further up the river from Stockton, and a more upper class area. Many was the time when I cycled there after my evening paper round and felt safe for a couple of hours listening to them talk with me about country life. However it was only for a few years because a stunning day came when Ken announced he had been offered a job in Africa. At that time, in 1956, it was a strange and wondrous thing that he had been offered and accepted a job at the Williamson's Diamond Mines in central Africa as an engineer. Maureen was to follow him after he got settled. Within months I was bereft of those evenings in Eaglescliffe but strangely comforted that my Uncle Ken had shown me the way, that the courage to make a dramatic move was possible, that it could be done, that it had been done by a man who cared for me, who had told me to keep on studying.

My father's other sister, Josie, had come from Ireland already married to a man from Galway with the same family name as us. His name was Myles and they had a council house at 30 Patterdale Avenue, with a small lawn at the front and a larger garden area at the back where Myles grew vegetables. They had children which gave me cousins, Kenneth, Cora and David. Myles worked at the chromium factory near Eaglescliffe and was proud of the fact that his work conditions had eroded away the membrane inside his nostrils. He was a good father, going to work every day, coming home every night, never going to the pubs or drinking with other men. In fact he wore a little pin in his shirt identifying him as a rare sort of Irishman, a Pioneer, one who had taken an oath never to let alcohol pass his lips, not even medicine or candy with alcohol in them. He kept that oath throughout all the years of his marriage. Though sadly for me it was not a house I was comfortable in when he was there. He would look at me with a strange sort of expression, not unfriendly but not friendly either. But I knew my Aunt Josie loved me and I loved her so I'd visit during the day

Survivor

when Myles was at work. I'd stop by after mowing my lawns and Josie would immediately start cooking bacon and eggs in a pan and raisin scones in the oven. It would have to be quickly done because we both knew without saying that I'd have to eat and be gone before Myles got home from work but the warmth of that kitchen and Josie and I talking about Ballybohan and people we knew there was an oasis of normalcy in my life. Josie was a happy and joyous person but it wasn't until years later that I realized when she was facing the stove, talking to me, and lifting her apron to wipe her eyes it was to hide from me the tears that she wept for me.

My schooldays at St. Mary's College were a world apart from my daily life. It was as if when I walked through the entrance to the school I was entering a safe place, blessed with the presence of the church and the priests, a place for me to be fed, a classroom environment of constant learning and daily challenges to my curiosity. Only in my first year did I get disciplined, twice being caned with a bamboo rod across my palms. Administered by the discipline master Father Byrnes, a tall thin stern faced priest with a craggy visage and authoritarian demeanor. He was also my Latin master and later I was to learn he was a man of understanding and compassion. I was caned because I had not completed my homework on two separate occasions. I did not resent my punishment. I knew it was deserved. I also knew it was impossible for me to try to explain the constant rain the night before and the crowded smoke filled library reading room and my favorite secluded bench in Ropner Park surrounded by a temporary flood. For it did rain often there in northern England and winter nights were long and dark and my strategy of finding places to read and do homework on nights I didn't have the comfort of sitting before a television in a warm room babysitting children in bed was at times difficult. I knew it was my fault the homework wasn't completed. I had a terrible fear the priests would find out about my home life and the beatings for I had a great shame that my father hit me and kicked me and that was a constant companion in those days. I couldn't help that I was a bastard and I hid that knowledge from everyone. I imagined all my schoolmates would shun me if they knew my parents weren't married when I was born. I thought I was

33

Survivor

the only one. I shivered internally at the thought of being found out and being expelled from the school and the loss of the education grant that gave me some relief from my father, a rock to stand on in the confidence I had something to barter.

After those canings I developed a different tactic. When I needed to I would arrive at the newsagents shop even before they had my canvas bag of newspapers ready and would race through my round and bike to school at full tilt standing on the pedals up off the seat so that I could reach the school a precious half hour before first class and I would creep into an empty class, or the back of the church if it was quiet, or even in desperation complete my homework sitting on a toilet seat in the boys bathroom, the door closed against my shame of having nowhere else to go. My strategies worked. I was never caught. I was never caned again.

The old man and woman who owned the small newsagents shop were always kind to me and always let me know they cared for me. I was their only boy to deliver newspapers and I'd have about thirty morning national newspapers to deliver up and down Yarm Road and surrounding streets and about forty deliveries of the local Evening Gazette in the evening. I had Sundays off because that's when the old man would walk the route with the big bulky Sunday newspapers collecting the payments for the week. On rainy days I'd cover myself and my newspaper bag with a thin yellow plastic coverall with a hood and even when raindrops would drip off my nose and the cardboard covering the holes in my shoes would get soggy I'd have a happy joy of accomplishment, a clean sort of joy, a completion twice a day of a task well done. I had spare cardboard and scissors beneath my books in my saddlebag and in those early morning hours I had a sense of being out and awake and working before most of the boys my age, being one with the men going to work and the women walking to their cleaning jobs like my mother. During winter in that far northern latitude my morning and evening deliveries would be under streetlights so I had a battery operated lamp attached to the front right strut of my bike and a dynamo operated rear red light with its power from a connection to the rear wheel. Fortunately even that far north the winters did not get much below freezing and my regular clothes

34

Survivor

with an additional shirt were enough to keep me warm. On the few times there would be a snowfall it would become an adventure and I'd tackle my route as a challenge that would bring happiness to my day. Then March would arrive and early morning light open up the world to me and I'd stand waiting for my early morning newspapers to be ready reveling in the thought that I'd have my homework done and the time to read the front pages of the newspapers I was delivering at stops on my route.

I'd become aware of the conflicts in government and society and knew that the newspapers I delivered represented different political opinions. I'd developed an open attitude, knowing we were working class and so therefore supporters of the Labour Party and was dimly beginning to understand the word socialism which to me meant mainly free medical care in the emergency room at the local hospital on Bowesfield Lane for cuts that needed stitches. It's a lonely time for a young boy to go to an emergency room by himself and lie that the wound was due to falling off a bike or being careless with a knife. I didn't confess those lies in confession for even to the priest I could not admit my father was hurting me. And in that way I began my first parting with the church I loved. The Times was the newspaper of the establishment, of the upper classes, somehow a superior sort of newspaper. I had several of those to deliver at large houses right on Yarm Road. Then about a half dozen of the Manchester Guardian, a newspaper I grew to recognize as progressive and socialist. Then there was the Telegraph and the Daily Express which I felt were the voice of the middle classes. And then of course were deliveries of the Daily Mirror, 'our' newspaper as it were, the newspaper of the working classes, racy and scandalous, but still containing articles on national and world news just as the other newspapers did. I began to see the descending quality of the writing in those newspapers. Even at the age of twelve the sheer volume of reading several hours a day had brought me to the point of being a critic of the writing of journalists. I have fond memories of my sister Patricia laughing and teasing me about my habit of reading from a book as I was walking down a street or road.

Survivor

I had become an indiscriminate reader of everything I could get my hands on. I knew that one day a light would dawn in my mind and I would escape. I was ready to embrace change, welcomed the thought of it, sought clues in everything I read, was willing to change my mind on learning new facts, and knew my Uncle Ken would expect me to keep going.

As the summer months of that year arrived, long days with only a few hours of total darkness at night, school vacation throughout the sunlit days, and the geography of my riding expanded. I was able to finish delivering the Evening Gazette just after five o'clock and could reach my Aunt Ivy and Uncle Bill in Bishop Auckland not long after six o'clock. It was a long fifteen mile ride north of Stockton with hills and mainly through countryside and I knew I'd be welcome in their house with my three younger cousins, Ernest, George, and Malcolm. My Aunt Ivy was my mother's older sister and had several times taken my mother and the rest of us into her home during times of crisis and madness on Derby Street, running away from my father, and though it would only be for several days to a week I remember vividly Aunt Ivy baking apple pies and lemon tarts to feast on after dinner while Uncle Bill was a gentle bear of a man who always had a giant jigsaw puzzle spread out on a large table for my cousins and me to work on.

There was a time when Aunt Ivy was recuperating from illness in the house at 21 Mill Street West, being cared for by her mother, and I remember her sitting up in bed with coverlets wrapped around her and she was helping me with the pronunciations of sentences from my French textbook. In that way I knew she was a woman with education and to be admired. I'd stay in Bishop Auckland until after sunset around eleven o'clock and then cycle back to Derby Street, stopping at points on clear nights, in sections where there were no street lights, to gaze up at the stars, to wonder at what I was learning from the astronomy books I'd read in passing through that section in Stockton Public Library on Wellington Street. I soon calculated that adding up my mileage for my paper route, and Bishop Auckland, that I was cycling close on forty miles for such a day and that whetted my appetite for more.

36

Survivor

My Aunt Ivy would always make me sandwiches to put into my saddle bag, usually of ham and cheese, wrapped in wax paper and in a brown paper bag and I knew my father and mother would not be home from the pubs until after eleven o'clock, and later if there was a stop at the fish and chips shop so I knew I could find drunken dangers by getting back too early. So I began to take a longer way back from Bishop Auckland, angling off on a road that would take me through the small town of Barnard Castle, a very upscale sort of tourist town, with a long history and Lord Barnard resident in his Castle as I would cycle past on the country lane. In that way I could increase my journey there and back to about forty miles and my total for the day to fifty miles, and more hours of peaceful isolation and daydreams of a better world, arriving back in Derby Street with the house in darkness and the final coals of the fire slumping into red embers, and me cuddling into my bed with old coats covering me and dreams of Ballybohan mixed with imaginations of what it would be like to be the son of a Lord.

Not that I was attracted to any sort of fantasies. I'd found a stall at the far end of Stockton market that sold used magazines and paperbacks and I'd discovered a love of science fiction. It was there every Wednesday and Saturday and the gruff old man that owned it sold those paperbacks at a low cost and even would take back two for one when I'd read them. I quickly developed distaste for fantasy and stories of magic and vampires. I knew they were ridiculous and I wanted reality in my life. For hard science fiction of space travel and technological advances, or even alternate worlds or time travel I was willing to accommodate myself to believably possible in a future far ahead. In that way while rejecting fantasies and impossibilities I was able to develop an additional daydream of escape that one day benevolent aliens could one day arrive and recognize what was in my mind and my heart and would take me away from Derby Street and give me tasks and projects worthy of merit, enable me to expand my mind, help me understand myself and the world around me. I already knew that I could learn quickly. At times of exams sometimes a whole page of what I'd read in a text book would flash into my mind as though written on a screen. At other times I'd feel myself just at the edge of comprehension in

37

Survivor

some difficult book from Stockton Public Library and I'd break out into a sweat, shivering, thinking that maybe my failure to follow on to the next paragraph was due to brain damage from my father kicking me in the head. For when I was trapped and thrown to the floor I'd cover my head with my arms and curl into a ball but even then my father would be able to attack me at my weakest points.

I have kept safe in my heart memory of three other people from that year, three people unrelated to me who showed me care and concern. One was the woman who owned a tobacco and candy shop on Yarm Road where I would deliver the Evening Gazette. Her name was Mrs. Gardner. When I would deliver the newspaper she would have me stop to talk with her, even if she had a customer she would beckon me to stay, and then she would question me on my school day, asking how I had done on one particular test or another, always keeping track, and she'd follow that by praising me and giving me a chocolate bar. I never found out if she knew of my Derby Street life but she treated me like a proud parent. It was the most praise I got from anyone during my school days. Her impact on my day to day life was profound.

The other person was a policeman. It came about after one night when I'd received a particularly terrifying beating, one in which I thought my father was going to kill me. After it was over and I was in bed, in tears, getting up and looking in a mirror and seeing my bruised eye and dried blood from my nose and lips, determination gripped me and I took the money I had secretly saved from my three sources of income and left the house and cycled through a deserted High Street, then on to Yarm and the country lane leading south to the Pennines, and across England, and a long way to Liverpool and the ferry ships across the Irish sea, heading for Dublin, then Roscommon and Ballybohan. I knew I had enough money for the ferry. It was after midnight when I set out. A couple of hours into me steady pedaling away a police car pulled over and stopped me. They took me and my bike back to Stockton Police Station where all I could confess to was where I lived. My tears had dried and I was hardened and ready for another beating. And then a wonderful thing happened. Even though the Police Station was only a short distance from Derby Street they took a long time to go get

Survivor

my parents. The policeman I remember brought me a big mug of milky cocoa and a thick sandwich of fresh buttered bread with chunks of tasty cheddar cheese and didn't question me further but just sat on the bench beside me with his arm around my shoulders as I ate and told me to take my time, there would be another sandwich if I wanted it. After a while he got up and went through a frosted glass door to the outer waiting room and I saw people were out there and I heard loud shouting voices. Then my father and mother came in and my father called me son and they took me home. I wasn't beaten. Thank you Mr. Policeman, I will remember and honor you all my life.

The third person I will always remember was another stranger. It had started out as a normal summer day with my father in a benevolent mood taking us all on a double-decker bus to just outside Yarm where we walked a path alongside the river to a beach crowded with families on beach towels, in bathing suits, picnicking and enjoying the sunshine. He called it Loch Leven though it was not actually a loch and was just a shallow wide section of the river. Some people were going out swimming and for some reason my father wanted to show how good he was at swimming and several times went out further than anyone else, waving back to us on the beach and challenging others to swim out to him. He then came back and picked me up and swam part of the way out and let go of me and shouted for me to swim back. I'd never been out of my depth before and never had swimming lessons. I panicked and managed to struggle back to shore. The next time my father took me out further. I went under a couple of times before my feet found the bottom and I again made it back to the shore. My father ignored my protests and my attempts to get away from him and took me out a third time. I thought I was going to be drowned. I thought he did it deliberately. I was too far from the shore. I was going under for the third time, choking on the water, when a man swam out from the beach and rescued me. I was lying on my back on the sand, coughing and choking, when that same man walked right up to my father and punched him an almighty wallop right on his nose. Then he walked away. All the way back on the bus, my father holding a towel to his bloody nose, I was a bastard once again, it was my entire fault. Thank you unknown stranger. I will remember you and honor you all my life.

Survivor

Chapter 3

As I entered the second form at St. Mary's College, moving from the first year classroom in the prefabricated buildings on the side of the school proper, into the long brick classrooms building, with a glass windowed corridor looking out onto the lawn with the Virgin Mary statue, beyond that the stone flagged exercise yard and the tall old oak tree flanking the gymnasium building, going beyond my twelfth birthday, I slowly became aware that there was a great deal more knowledge in the world for me to tackle. It was an awareness that would expand as the years passed.

In the days of Ballybohan I had imagined that all I had to do was keep reading and a day would come when I would have read everything worth reading, leaving only scraps and shreds of things to collect. In my days of the junior library reading and rereading the collection of children's books I had been proud of my accomplishment, as though I had climbed a mountain and reached the top. When I had got over my amazement at the thousands upon thousands of books crowding the shelves of the adult library and set myself the task of reading it all in the years ahead, looking to escape from my fears, I had felt that all the knowledge in the world was there for me to find. Now it was if my mind had expanded into a realization that there was not a limit to knowledge and books, that there would always be more to explore, that I need not fear I would reach the end and not reach what I was looking for. It did not daunt me. It encouraged me. I had found a new horizon.

The science classes were taught by lay teachers which seemed proper to me. In mathematics class I went through the chapter exercises on algebra with happiness inside me, geometry and proofs and using my protractor set enthralled me, calculations using logarithms appealed to my sense of precision, beginning calculus puzzled me but made me wonder why I had not thought of such a concept before, sines and cosines and tangents and ladders leaning against walls and billiard balls colliding with inelastic and elastic collisions at precise angles on green baize billiard tables populated my thoughts as I delivered newspapers and fell asleep

41

Survivor

beneath old coats giving me a comfort and purpose that was a bulwark against the hits and blows and bruises of my daily life.

In my first classes in chemistry with Mr. Bradley it was as if it was knowledge that had been waiting for me. The periodic table and the elements seemed so much common sense and the descriptions of atoms and electrons and ions and protons and neutrons captured me and I spent hours and meticulous care drawing electron orbitals as if they were planets whirling around a nucleus, not that we had been assigned it but I had wanted to do it. We had simple experiments and one day Mr. Bradley asked us to bring samples of tap water from home so we could work out if our taps were delivering hard water or soft water. Mr. Bradley was a kind and softly spoken bear of a man so I couldn't explain to him my fears of my father and Derby Street so I cheated and got a small bottle of water from my grandmother's house on Mill Street West and marked it as being from Derby Street. That sin haunted me for a long time but I didn't know how to put it right and it must have put into me a resolve not to ever do such a thing again. Chemistry became my favorite subject. It seemed to me to be so sensible and logical and coherent, facts building on facts, direct information about the world around me. Avogadro's number and the laws of constant proportion, and descriptions of the properties of elements brought a reality into my life that had been missing, became a bedrock foundation to my perceptions of the land and roads and buildings I cycled through, became a confidence of knowing that remained with me and grew with me as the years passed and grew with the chemistry I learned, always willingly and always wanting more.

Physics with Mr. Jeavons was another part of the day I looked forward to, with tall glass windows spilling sunlight into that laboratory classroom, with a long chart of the electromagnetic spectrum along the top of one wall, with experiments and calculations in magnetism, and electricity, and optics. I fell in love with Physics just as I had done with Chemistry. It also seemed so logical and easy to learn, indeed hard to forget, travelling with my thoughts as the days went by and weeks went into months and on into summer, knowing there would be no end to learning, looking

Survivor

ahead into the textbook, apprehensive about my ability to comprehend what was yet to come, looking back at pages that had become comprehensible and sensible, feeling confidence, putting distance between me and my father, knowing I must keep my learning a secret, thoughts of the red hot poker and reading again and being blinded still having the power to set my heart thudding against my ribs, causing me to stand up on the pedals of my bike and pedal faster and faster as if to escape the stinging in my eyes.

I'd tell Mrs. Gardner how well I'd done on my exams and thank her for my chocolate bar but I'd never tell her exactly how well I'd done. That was a secret I kept close to myself, that often I got the top mark in the class and sometimes way above my classmates, that frightened me my father would find out, as I took my term report card and hid it in my saddle bag, and sat on my favorite bench in Ropner Park and forged my parents signatures to take it back to school the next day. I was never caught, never found out.

English classes were at once easy and a puzzle to me. It wasn't as if I needed to study. There were separate classes in English literature and English grammar. In the literature classes we were assigned books to read chapter by chapter. I disobeyed that instruction. Like all the fiction books I took out from Stockton Public Library, still consuming about two a day, and the second hand science fiction books I purchased on the Stockton market, once I started reading all I wanted was to find a quiet place where I would not be disturbed until I had read the book to the very end. I had no thought of how fast I was reading, no means of comparing myself to others, so I read in disobedience to my teacher Father Carroll and didn't study but just responded to questions when I was asked in class and didn't volunteer anything additional so my having read an entire book in the days after assignment wasn't detected. English grammar classes were quite a different matter. I had no problems identifying nouns and adjectives and verbs and adverbs, after all I was learning those categories of language in my Latin classes, but the classification of other components seemed to be a grab bag of words that had no impact on me so I just mentally shrugged and followed the rules when taking tests. So much of

English corresponded to Latin that I felt a familiarity with both, quite unlike my feelings with Irish, which I still practiced, saying my prayers at night in Irish, counting in Irish, imaging to myself the Irish words for things around me, writing my name in the Irish language in secret places.

When it came to writing essays for class assignments I discovered that only myself and another classmate, Dennis Lyons, were getting the top marks and even then way above the other students. It seemed to me to be natural for that to be so. The writing came easily to me. I liked Dennis. He was tall and fair haired with blue eyes and a smooth pale complexion, always very clean, always smelling as if his clothes were freshly washed, and so very handsome to my eyes.

Up to that point I'd only thought people I was related to were good looking. I'd actually thought most English people to be quite ugly and even possibly might smell bad if I got too close to them. Blue eyes like ours seemed to identify us and brown eyes in people caused me to withdraw from them and not want to be near them. Later in that second year another student arrived from Ireland and became not only my good friend but also got top marks in essays in English classes so with Dennis Lyons we became the top three students in English with the rest of the students trailing far behind. The boy from Ireland was called Luke Casey and he was from Ballina in Mayo and he had younger brothers Thomas and Patrick. He had black hair and blue eyes and was also very tall and very good looking. I was often invited to his house in a street just off Yarm road where at times it seemed as if I had been transported back to Ireland. I welcomed those times and wished so much that I had been part of a family like that, happy and working together.

I enjoyed my classes in Latin and in French but I was a constant despair to my teachers, Father Byrnes teaching Latin and Father Green teaching French. They were both from Ireland and their voices fell gently on my ears and I wanted to please them but somehow I found it difficult to separate Latin from French and would write in a mixture of both so I was not a very good student in tests, falling about the middle of the class and sometimes even lower. I did however like it on days when Father Byrnes would challenge us one at a time to stand and read a paragraph from a Latin text then translate it into English. I loved the sonorous sentences and managed to stumble through the translation adequately enough, enjoying Gallicis Reribus and the bravery of the Celtic tribes of mainland Europe. It did arouse in me the desire to read about Roman times and that led to learning about the Roman occupation of Britain and that Hadrian's Wall was just thirty miles north of Stockton, that being about the limit of Roman rule. It was a period when I paused in my rigid schedule of reading nonfiction books in alphabetical sequence in the Stockton Public Library. I enjoyed several months reading about the Celtic tribes in England and the coming of the Saxons and the Viking invasions. That didn't help me in my history classes in which I had surely the position of the worst student in the class. It didn't help that my lay teacher, Mr. Howe, was a short sighted man with an upper class accent and lisp that I found funny and not likeable. It also didn't help that the history books were in conflict with the histories I had learned in Ireland and were at odds with the small green book my grandfather had given me, published in 1870 and called A Catechism of the History of Ireland, Ancient and Modern, by William J. O'Neill Daunt. That to me was the real history and Mr. Howe was teaching distortions and falsehoods and Oliver Cromwell was an evil scoundrel and the horror of the Famine had been caused entirely by the English trying to kill all the Irish people and sending them on coffin ships, sailing the north Atlantic, dead bodies tossed overboard for the sharks following all the way, so many dead that if there was a gravestone on the north Atlantic for the Irish eaten by the sharks then it would be possible to walk from Ireland to America. But Mr. Howe would have none of this and his red pen was scribbled all over my exercise books as I stubbornly used the catechism of the history of Ireland to tell him of his errors and guilt in the complicity of English history. He did give me one hilarious indelible memory when one day a student placed a mouse on the ledge above the blackboard and as it scurried to and fro with its tail dangling down short sighted Mr. Howe would helplessly try to rub the tail away with the board duster, the whole class roaring with laughter each time. The mouse survived. I survived. English history remained unchanged.

I had another remarkable memory from Latin class with Father Byrnes. It was a warm sunny afternoon and I had that lunch time walked down the road to buy a bag of broken biscuits at Woolworths. I was so very hungry that day, more so than usual. I began to feel queasy as I sat doing a translation with Father Byrnes sitting at his desk marking exercises, the stack of blue books in front of him. I raised my hand to ask for permission to stand and go to the toilet. He didn't notice me. Over the next few minutes I tried frantically to attract his attention but without success so I then took the bold step of standing up without permission and walking up to him at the front of the classroom. As he looked up at me, his glasses making him seem as intimidating as his position as discipline master warranted it was as if the world had fallen on me and I became dizzy and disoriented and hot and cold at the same time and to my horror projectile vomited all over the desk and the exercise books and Father Byrnes' cassock. The minutes after that were hazy but I found myself lying on a couch in the study Father Byrnes had at the end of the hallway and he was bathing my face and pushing me back down as I tried to get up and saying soothing words and calming my panic. While all my classmates thought I was being punished and caned I experienced quite the opposite, finding depths of compassion in that kindly priest, making me stay there that for the rest of that afternoon, having weak milky tea brought to me, checking up on me frequently, making sure I was recovered by the end of the school day to go home, his caring worried eyes following me as I got on my bike and slowly rode off down the road.

Father Green, my other Irish priest, my French language master, who later was to be my form master, took me aside a few days later and told me to go to him if I was ever in trouble and spent time with me explaining differences between French and Latin and assuring me that in time it would all sort itself out. So in that same week I found both those priests were my allies that would stand by me, that they were more than just my teachers.

Survivor

There are people who like books. I liked books from the very beginning. In holding them and turning pages, reading on and on, becoming submerged in them. And so from my first years at St. Mary's College they were central to my life. I had been quickly sorted out in the first few months. I had only one class in music. The thirty of us were told to stand and sing 'De you ken John Peel'. I didn't have a clue what the teacher was saying as my classmates enthusiastically burst into a loud song which baffled me. I'd never heard the song before. I'd never been taught to sing. So I stood near the back of the classroom and opened and closed my mouth in what I thought would be an approximation of what I was hearing so as to pretend I was singing. That was my first and last class.

Similarly in art class I was given a large sheet of paper and some paints and told to paint a picture that represented 'the last of the Mohicans'. I had a dim image that was to do with American Indians so I carefully painted a standing warrior complete with feather headdress from head to heels. I'd never painted or drawn before. Such activities were for other kids, not us. That was my first and last art class. I believe that all children when very young should be given presents to stimulate interest in drawing and painting and singing. I was not. I'd passed through that window of childhood where those talents develop. It is still sadness for me, regret for what could have been.

That was how I finished up with a full class schedule with classes in English Literature, English Grammar, French, Latin, Religious Instruction, History, Mathematics, Physics, and Chemistry. There were exercises and sports on two afternoons a week. I was to be with them for five years. I had shorter periods of instruction in Geography and ancient Greek. I was preparing for the Ordinary General Certificate of Education, my 'O' Level GCEs as we would talk among ourselves. We had five years ahead, internal tests and exams until then, but the weeks would come, being tested on our knowledge, with the tests designed outside the school, coming from the northern universities, given on the same day at the same time throughout the country, sealed and anonymous, a set length of time to complete, sent away and graded anonymously so there would be no bias, just as it had been for the eleven plus, I had

47

Survivor

a chance, I had the books, I had my bike, I liked the teachers, that is except for the history teacher Mr. Howe who for some peculiar reason always gave me low marks for my version of history. I knew whoever would be grading my GCE test papers would not know I was working class, would not know I was born a bastard.

I always felt different from the other boys, part of that coming from having to hide the fact that I was a bastard and my father was hitting me, some because of my perception that my classmates were English, another part coming from a lack of interest in football or cricket, thinking that kicking a ball from one end of a field to another or batting away a ball in front of a wicket was so pointless, rather like running in place and going nowhere. Now running on our rare cross country runs and cycling somewhere were quite a different matter. They were exercises in going places, enjoying the winds and breezes in my face, taking great deep breaths of the air, my lungs feeling strong and vigorous. They were real to me, exercise that was an accomplishment. But that feeling of being different remained with me despite my friendships with my classmates and was to trouble me for years to come, not knowing why I felt that way, wanting to be just like my friends, wanting to share in their passions and their world. But it was not to be. It was something waiting for me in the future.

In the meantime it was the nature of things that several boys at a time would find reasons to enjoy being together, having temporary interests to explore, having lunch together, talking and comparing notes, but it was not in any sense exclusive or even permanent, changing throughout the years. I have no memories of strife or hostility or exclusiveness among any of my classmates. It was enough that we all had a common identity, in our St. Mary's College uniforms, striving together for our GCEs, that concepts of interpersonal rivalries had no place in our world. Even at the very worst time for me on one day when I had to go to school in misery because my father had punished me by cutting my hair into patches and tufts, I only endured the unwelcome attentions of my classmates, crowding around me to look, for one morning, and even then it was not unkind or mocking, just intense curiosity, as though I had undergone some peculiar accident or calamity. So feeling

48

Survivor

different was something that would come and go. It did cause me to leave out the entire section of books on psychology in my journey throughout my methodical perusal of the non-fiction section of the Wellington Street adult library, as though I feared what I might find there, that there was something terribly wrong with me, something I would not be able to endure, something that would plunge me into utter despair.

I did get to visit the homes of some of my classmates, experiencing a normality for life I had not had since Ballybohan. Luke Casey's family in Stockton, near Yarm Road on my paper route, gave me the comfort of an Irish family. They had moved to Stockton from Ballina in Mayo in Ireland. Luke had two brothers, Tom and Patrick. Peter Wadsworth was the son of a greengrocer in Middlesbrough and they lived above the store. He had a wonderful father who had taken a small room in the back yard and cleaned it and whitewashed the walls and made it empty and dust free so that Peter could make a reflector telescope. Peter had the ambition to make a six inch reflector telescope and his father bought him the books and equipment and the glass blanks to grind, the various grades of carborundum, the brass tube and the eyepiece, and encouraged him to go ahead. And Peter did, assiduously and persistently for month after month, as I would visit and watch in amazement and awe. Peter had pictures and drawings of the planets and star charts all over the walls of his bedroom and by the time the telescope was finished and he and his father and I saw the craters on the moon, and Mars as a reddish disc, and Saturn's rings, and the starry night sky, I had become entranced with astronomy and my life had another foundation, curiously enough melding with my reading my second hand science fiction paperbacks.

By the time I was thirteen I had managed to live well enough, always moving, always on the go, going though the angers and violence of my father by treating it as an inevitable sort of thing, unpredictably ranging from stormy days to relatively calm days. My bruises healed quickly. My heart and dreams and imaginations were not quenched. My learning was not stopped. The threat of the red hot poker was on the periphery of my thoughts but I had gained the confidence that Martin and the other Irishmen from the pub

49

would tell my father to leave the boy alone, as they did often enough when they'd see him hit me or call me names. So that confidence accreted around me and protected me. By the time I was thirteen and a half I was thrilled to know of Sputnik orbiting earth and beeping radio signals for weeks. In those early weeks of a cold October 1957 I lifted up my thoughts to space. I grew up, I began to imagine the future of space exploration.

I was beginning to lose my Irish. It was as if it was falling away from me. It was as if I was feeling the sadness of loss because by that time I'd known that my grandfather had died and in some way they were inextricably part of a completed part of my life. So as the words and sentences and phrases were lost to me I anguished at their loss and tried to hang on to them as they vanished from my lips but remained in my heart.

In that environment of learning I was innocent of my future yet to come so thought little beyond passing the term tests and examinations. It was a happy time for me despite the turmoil back in Derby Street. And even among that turmoil there were oases of armistice. As on one Spring weekend my father and some other Irishmen took me in an open topped truck to fields outside town where we were to hoe rows of mangels, a sort of turnip for cows I was told. The air was fresh and seeing the long rows of seedlings stretching in rows across acres of land I felt a special kind of happiness, kept only to myself, for the purity of that happiness, that it remained intact with me, adding to my store of many such other identifications with nature. My father's friend Martin showed me how to hoe the seedlings, swing the hoe just in such a manner that only single seedlings roughly six inches apart should remain. Martin was the fastest and most efficient of the men hoeing the mangels. He walked down the rows almost in a lazy slow walk swinging the hoe as if it were the simplest thing in the world. He was far faster than the other men. At one point the farmer went to look at Martin's rows and came back smiling and nodding. He was paying by the row and Martin was efficiently placing the seedlings at just the right separation. After several days of that I was managing to get several rows done a day and at a shilling a row. Martin would check my work before the farmer did and would tidy

50

up sections where I had left two seedlings, propping up any seedling that had fallen on its side. I was well paid, and wonder of wonders my father did not try to take it from me. Martin and the other Irishmen would watch the transaction from the farmer, looking out for me, protecting me, for the farmer was English and they wanted to make sure I was getting what I was due, and being a boy, needed their protection against the English. To me it had the added benefit of protecting me from my father, knowing that at the worse, at home, he'd be satisfied with just half of it to add to what he had earned and I could finagle so that he'd get the poorer part of it, satisfied that he'd go drink his and mine would go for food and Mam and Pat and Mary and Thomas and Terrence could have cod and chips with lots of scraps for 'Tommy' and 'Terry' and their part of the food made up for them, a few succulent pieces of fried cod with chips and scraps, on their own little boat of newspaper.

The next few years went by in much the same manner as I grew taller and more confident, continuing my exploration of the nonfiction shelves of the Wellington Street Public library, until the days came when it was time to take the General Certificate of Education 'O' levels. The gymnasium had been cleared and chairs with a swing up writing surface placed far enough apart so that proctors could see if any student would try to cheat from another student, not that that was something most of us would even attempt to do, imbued with the honor and integrity of our daily contact with the priests and Latin and Mass and religious classes. I was several months past sixteen and I looked forward to that week of change in my life. I knew that after I passed the exams I would get to concentrate on only three subjects for two years, going on into the lower Sixth and upper Sixth, becoming treated special because of that status.

I was filled with mixed emotions of anticipation, anxiety, and an upsurge of confidence each day, knowing the blue books of written answers would be collected and taken away to another part of England where unknown people would evaluate my answers and essays, where the grading would be done without bias or prejudice, them not knowing the answers were written in a working class area, in a Catholic school, by a bastard boy, beaten and hit often by his

Survivor

father. The weeks after became a happy sort of time, enjoying the warmer weather promising of a summer holiday, our classes being more of a review of the years that had gone before, waiting for the results to be returned to the school. When the day came for the headmaster, Father Trueman, to tell each of us how well we had done I was excited and overwhelmed to find out that I had passed in seven out of my eight subjects, failing only in history, that last one not even troubling me, thinking of it as a badge of honor, that I had failed an exam in the English version of history and therefore of no consequence at all. My entry into the lower Sixth was assured.

There was one day of sheer fright for me. Father Trueman sent word to about ten of us who had been the very best students for that year, passing with seven or eight 'O' levels. We were told to assemble in the library in the main house by the church where a reporter and photographer from the Evening Gazette would be taking a group photograph. It would be our last day of the school year. That raised in me a panic, my heart beating fast, my face flushed, trembling, fearing my father seeing the picture in the Evening Gazette, frightened he would know I had done well, would attack me again, would threaten me again. So I ran. I split off from my classmates and ran to my bike and cycled rapidly away, not giving any opportunity for anyone to stop me. For the next week I cycled everywhere in a constant ferment of fear, not even telling Mrs. Gardner how well I had done. I did confide in my sister Patricia and my Aunt Josie and my mother knowing they would keep the news from my father and so in that way the weeks of the summer went by and I relaxed thinking that particular crisis had gone by.

At that point all my father knew was that I would be returning to school in September so that I could take another G.C.E. 'O' level exam. I had agreed with Father Green that I should retake the history exam so that my record would be complete. I tackled my repugnance and went back to my textbooks and forced myself to learn the lies of the English history and did indeed pass when November came. By that time I was studying my chosen three subjects of Chemistry, Physics, and Mathematics, looking forward

52

Survivor

to two years of preparing for the Advanced level of the General Certificate of Education; my G.C.E. 'A' levels.

A few days after I got the news of passing the history exam my constructed world fell in ruins about me. It was as if my lies about history had turned around and were punishing me. I'd returned to Derby Street after a cycle ride to visit my friend John Green in Dormanstown, swapping science fiction paperbacks, happy that I had a new record in the half hour ride from his house to Stockton High Street, thinking I'd go to bed before my father and mother would get home from the pub. I had miscalculated. I was punched as soon as I wheeled my bike into the hallway, my mother and sisters and brothers screaming and shouting as he punched me and kicked me and reviled me again and again and again. It seemed as if it went on for hours. He had found out about my exam results. I wasn't going to be allowed to continue going to school. I was going to go dig ditches like him. I was going to work like him. I was a bastard. My reading days were over. That would be beaten out of me.

Early the following morning before I left the house for my paper round my mother told me to meet her at the Empire cinema, where she cleaned the cinema floors, after I finished my paper round. I was extremely miserable and unhappy. I'd begun to think of running away but I had nowhere to run to. I knew I'd be taken back home for even more of the same treatment. To my surprise my mother told me she was going to go to the school with me to talk with the priests. That amazed me. I'd never known my mother to get on a bus before. When we reached the school she went in to talk with Father Trueman and Father Green in the headmaster's study while I sat in the kitchen with the housekeeper and was given milky cocoa and chunky cheddar cheese sandwiches. I could hear the sound of my classmates in the building. I didn't know what was going on. I couldn't work out a way to escape my misery. At one point Father Green came out and looked right at me and said "we thought you were accident prone". I cried inside. My brave mother was telling the priests about my father hitting me. She would get hit if he found out. I felt an overwhelming need to protect her and knew I could not. I felt helpless. A long while later my mother

53

Survivor

came out, holding a letter in her hands, and Father Green came and sat with me and explained the letter was to my father asking him to wait a while until Father Trueman could contact someone he knew who could get me a job in a laboratory in the Imperial Chemical Industry in Billingham where I could earn just as much as digging ditches. Father Green held my hands in his as tears flooded my eyes and told me to be brave and told me in the soft cadence of Ireland that I loved so much that as a laboratory assistant I.C.I. would pay for me to go to night school at a technical college where I could still study for my 'A' levels and though it may take me longer it could still be done. He was very kind and kept talking to me, convincing me this was a way out, while insisting to me that I had the courage to accept my changed future, that they had written in the letter to my father about his 'illness' and why a laboratory job would bring in just as much money to the household. A kind fiction to hide their sadness at knowing the bruises and split lips and complaints of hurting ribs of prior years had now been explained to them by my Protestant mother. I knew she did it out of love and pride in me and I feared for her taking such a risk of enraging my father. But somehow she had known of the power of a letter from the priests addressed to my father promising that I could earn a regular good income. He did not rage when we returned home that day.

My world had changed. I had to get ready for an interview at I.C.I. in my immediate future. The time went by quickly as I tried to learn as much chemistry as possible, knowing each day was precious, that soon it would be the day to say goodbye to my classmates.

Survivor

Chapter 4

Imperial Chemical Industries in Billingham was the largest chemical company in England and one of the largest in the world. The place I had my interview was in a building close to the bus sheds. I'd dressed as clean and proper as I could with the school tie and a white shirt then walked to the end of Wellington Street by 7:45 in the morning where I'd been told to get on one of the red double-decker buses stopping at the bus stand. I had to look out for the destination Billingham ICI on the front of the bus for there were many other buses with different destinations at that busy time of the morning, thousands of workers crowding the High Street, an apprehension and excitement for me that I might actually get a job working in a laboratory and not have to go digging ditches.

The bus was already almost full when I got on so I wedged myself into a seat on the upper deck and looked out onto Norton Road as more stops were made, passing the elementary school and St. Mary's Church where I had prepared for my eleven plus, through Portrack where my Aunt Annie, my mother's sister, and my English cousins lived, and the five or six miles after that was all new to me, passing through Norton, down a bank and across meadows and a few buildings, then up another bank into Billingham where I became more apprehensive seeing the I.C.I. office buildings and tall towers and massive pipes stretching from the road off into the distance.

It seemed as if there were dozens of buses converging on the bus sheds inside the factory gates, more people hurrying to work than I'd ever seen before, comparable to the crowds on market days on Stockton High Street but around the bus sheds these were all adults and mainly men. It was a cold day and dark and overcast and street lights were still on because it was early December. The sun had yet to rise.

I wasn't even quite sure what an interview would involve, whether I would have to do tests or what, or be questioned on my GCE knowledge. The kind gruff man who greeted me as I entered his office set me at ease. It wasn't an interrogation at all. He talked of Father Trueman and St. Mary's College, told me I had a good number of 'O' levels and that I could go to night school at the local Stockton-Billingham Technical College and that I could get something called day release. I didn't ask any questions. I was consumed with a passion imbued in me by my chemistry teacher, Mr. Alf Bradley, who had advised me to insist that I wanted a laboratory job and not an office job. At one point I felt as if I were in an unreal situation and the man talking to me was very tiny as if my eyes were about to fail me. I was very hungry. I'd only had a cup of tea before leaving Derby Street. Then as suddenly as it had begun he walked me to the door telling me I'd get a letter on when and where I would report to work.

When I got outside the street lights were off and the sun had come up and I walked from the bus sheds down the road out of ICI to a row of shops where I bought a cup of tea and an egg sandwich and sat on a bench at the bus stop waiting for a bus to Stockton. My eyes had come back to normal and I had a growing sense of belonging. I felt I was going to meet more men like the nice man who had interviewed me, men like my Uncle Ken.

The letter, when it arrived, on embossed cream ICI notepaper, with an ICI embossed envelope, addressed to me, John Fahey, 35 Derby Street, Stockton-on-Tees, was my ticket into the future. I was told to report for work in the main laboratory on the ground floor of 'O' building at 8:15 am on January 1, 1961. The letter included the salary of £285 a year to be paid once a month. I was to report to the Personnel office on the afternoon of my first day.

It wasn't unusual at that time for New Years Day in England to be a working day. Christmas Day and the day after, Boxing Day, were holidays. In Scotland to the north it was the other way around with Christmas Day a working day and New Years Day a holiday. Since Tees-side had in earlier centuries been closer in many ways to Scotland the final week of December had a general celebratory air with full pubs and shops and people enjoying a good time and that was the atmosphere in which I prepared for my first job. Even my father seemed to be amazed and conciliatory toward me. "That's five pounds 48 a week", he said, looking up from the pencil and paper he'd done his calculation on, "pity you only get it once a month", and he gave me back my precious embossed ICI letter. My

Survivor

heart sank. I'd already calculated 23 pounds 75 pence a month and I was sure the prospect of that much treasure would cause my father to demand and take as much of that as he could.

I had to end my paper delivery job but I did work until the last day I could; in the final week taking the new boy around the delivery route. I arranged with Mr. and Mrs. Roe that my sister Patricia would take over the baby sitting job though by that time the babies had grown into active chattering girls and they had moved to a bungalow on Norton High Street. It was in that bungalow where I'd received an unusual compliment one night when Mr. Roe's parents had returned to the house with them. The TV was off and I was completing my Latin homework when the older Mr. Roe looked at me collecting my translation and books and gave me a half crown to add to my babysitting payment and sighed and said: "I wish you were my son." It seemed strange to me at the time, especially with his grown son standing there but Arthur didn't seemed at all bothered by it and that night and from then on, instead of me getting a late night bus from Norton to Stockton, he drove me back into Stockton, dropping me off at the end of Derby Street, on Wellington Street.

My lawn mowing work I did keep. I could do that on weekends or evenings, whenever the weather allowed, and I did enjoy the peaceful feelings I got pushing the reel mower and trimming the edges of the lawns. The old ladies complimented me on my new job and gave me extra shillings to start me on my way.

From my first day of work I had a sort of enlightenment. I had the same emotions I'd gone through on arriving in Ballybohan when I was a child. It was still dark but there were street lights and brilliant lights mounted on the sides of laboratory buildings. The letter had told me I was to report for work in the main laboratory on the ground floor of 'O' Building at 8:15 in the morning. I walked from the bus sheds into the complex of large two and three and four storey brick laboratory buildings with large windows, asking directions from the throng of men and women walking rapidly past me. I was walking into another world. I had the title Laboratory Assistant, people were kind to me, helping me, and when I arrived

Survivor

in the main laboratory I was spoken to by my proper name, and there were wonders all around me to explore.

I was first assigned to a very old man, shorter than myself, who explained to me that I would assist him in his work dissolving small fragments of material with aqua-regia in platinum crucibles, gently warmed and cooled when necessary. Those solutions were to be diluted and samples tested for various reasons. He would explain to me as I helped him. Mr. Rudd I think his name was, though on that I could be wrong, but then I was still only 16 and hadn't yet learned to write down people's names who had an influence on my life. Mr. Rudd had a ready smile, and eyes that were creased from laughter, kind and calling me John, and telling me I must learn to be careful, and precise, and keep good documentation in the lab book he gave me. He sat me at a beautiful precision balance in a glass case with the front to slide up to weight the samples. As he guided me weighing out samples, the platinum crucible first on the right hand pan, and brass weights taken from a felt lined polished dark wood box, each weight having its own cavity within the box, everything handled with tweezers, carefully, precisely on the left hand pan, balancing the pans, then do the whole thing all over again with a small fragment of solid material in the platinum crucible. I was able to follow his directions as he talked. He told me that after lunch I had to go to the personnel office, and they would tell me I could become a day-release Laboratory Assistant by promising to sign up at the local Stockton-Billingham Technical College for two evenings and a full day which would be my day release day and it would be on full pay with my books and tuition paid for so long as I got good grades and come to work regular five days a week on days when you don't have school, and come on John lad you've done enough weighing for this morning, let's go to the cafeteria and I'll buy you lunch today because you don't have your badge yet which you'll use in future to buy a ticket from the lady at that booth over there, it's ten pence over there, you can have as much of everything as you want, seeing that you are not yet eighteen.

I do remember Mr. Rudd well and how he made me feel. It was a very different world from Ballybohan as we walked through the laboratory buildings and up a walkway, through the green metal

Survivor

fencing defining the limits of the laboratory buildings area, to cross a crowded parking lot to a huge two storey company cafeteria located in front of a main road. I could see as we walked by huge buildings without windows along the road and overhead pipes of different colors and that all being repeated at further and further distances over what I was told stretched over across the Tees and there are buses on the roads through the factory and I was to take one the following day after reporting to Mr. Rudd and I'd get to see the original farmhouse in the middle of the factory set in lawns and now a medical clinic where I would get my medical examination.

So in that enlightenment on that first day I had the same emotions reminding me of Ballybohan, the sky full of light, the air so fresh, the good food, the kindness, the wonders, being called by my proper name.

I'd already begun willingly to adjust to this new world. Calling the midday meal lunch seemed awkward to me since in the working class it was called dinner. I'd already known that but discovered it was just the same kind of meal I'd had at St. Mary's College under a different name. In that long cafeteria building with dining rooms upstairs for executives I followed Mr. Rudd and took a tray and cutlery and moved into the line behind him as I selected from a wide variety of hot meats and fish, adding vegetables as I moved along the line, adding near the end of the line apple pie and hot custard before reaching the cashier where on following days I would hand over my ten pence ticket. I was urged by Mr. Rudd to fill my plate, reminding me of my grandfather in Ballybohan, and I was filled with gratitude and the urge to do the right thing. We took our trays over to a table where he knew other people from 'O' Building and I was accepted among them and introduced as the new lad from Stockton. I was shy and on the verge of nervousness but they made me feel comfortable and I didn't have to answer any questions that would make me flush and reveal the fears of my daily life.

When we walked out into the sunshine Mr. Rudd turned left, away from the way we'd come in: "come on John", he said "I'll show you some more things. We have enough time": As we walked he pointed out the bus stand on the main road where I would be

59

Survivor

getting the Corporation bus to my day-release school and told me that on days when I had night school I was to leave the laboratory at four thirty instead of five o'clock so that I could have another meal before going to classes. He called that meal dinner. He showed me the adjoining building that showed short lunch time films about industry and safety, for free, and then a small shop where I could get a haircut, another adjacent pub for men who wanted a pub lunch with a beer. Beyond that was a huge green level field with goal posts at one end for sports and recreation. The pub was called the Synthonia pub, short for synthetic ammonia and it all belonged to I.C.I. and only for I.C.I. employees and within a long perimeter metal fence separating it from the main road.

At that I felt the wonders would never cease. After Mr. Rudd walked me back and across the parking lot to a small one storey prefabricated building painted white, for my personnel meeting, making sure I'd know the way back to 'O' Building, telling me to be sure to return before it would be time to go home. At that my thought was that I never wanted to go back home to be hit and beaten and called you bastard. I'd be happy to live there. I just needed a place to sleep and keep my bike. I already felt I had a new home. Everyone called me John. But it was just a passing fantasy and I let it go as I entered the personnel office.

That afternoon continued in the same light of discovery. The personnel man was kind and friendly, taking his time to explain the documents I was signing. He even joked with me at the beginning, telling me it was a historic day because the farthing was no longer legal tender. I hadn't seen that tiny quarter penny coin for a long time and he put me at ease by laughing and saying I'd have no need of that anymore anyway. I told him I wanted to do my 'A' Levels in Chemistry, Physics, and Mathematics and he nodded approvingly, saying that with my 'O' level results it would be very easy for me. He advised me to take a combined 'A' level in Mathematics, with Pure Mathematics and Applied Mathematics together, and I.C.I. would pay for them with good grades on my part. He gave me a syllabus book for Stockton-Billingham Technical College and more forms to fill out that I would take to register for the soon to begin classes. He urged me to do it the following day after I reported to

60

Survivor

work, letting my supervisor know I needed a few hours off to do it. He explained the Corporation buses went by every twenty minutes and it would take less than twenty minutes on the bus through the streets to Billingham town center where the college was. He told me many of my teachers were likely part time I.C.I. people and they would look after me and that many of my classmates would also be day-release students. Then he turned to telling me about my pay and my heart surged with excitement. One of the forms I'd signed I had to take to the bank on the main road just outside the factory gate because my monthly pay would be deposited there and I'd be given a bank book and a cheque book. I'd get a pay slip accounting for my salary and deductions delivered to the laboratory every month. I was thrilled to hear the word salary instead of wages and my heart surged to find out that I wouldn't be getting a wage packet with money in it each week like others got, avoiding a weekly fight with my father demanding I give it to him. I declined an offer of an advance, knowing I had enough cash to get me through the first month. It made me feel quite posh, having a salary and a cheque book. By then I wanted to run back to Mr. Rudd and show him my papers and tell him about my personnel interview and it wasn't until I was running back to 'O' Building that the final information penetrated. To add to all of those gifts I was to be immediately eligible for the annual I.C.I. bonus as a percentage of my salary based upon the profit of the company in the previous year and that the bonus would be invested in I.C.I. voting stock that would be held in trust for me until I was twenty one.

When I got back to Mr. Rudd he entertained me with thoughts of previous years when he told me the bonus had been exceptionally good and that's why I should do a good job. I was determined to be the best Laboratory Assistant in 'O' Building, already anchored into the foundation of Chemistry, just wanting to be the best at everything. When I arrived back in Derby Street that evening it was already dark and the street lights were on, my mother was cooking bacon and eggs with baked beans on the stove, with bags of chips from the fish and chip shop being kept warm in the oven. As I recounted my day to my mother and Patricia, both of them smiling at me and happy for me, my father sat poking the coal

61

Survivor

fire listening to me, gruffly interrogating me to convince himself
that I really wouldn't be getting paid until the end of January. I was
tense at that but he didn't curse at me or lift his hand to me. Mary
was quiet as always, sitting beautiful and small. The little boys
Tommy and Terry were out playing in the street. As we were eating
my father told me that since I was now a man I was to have the
front parlor room to myself, moving out from the upstairs room I
shared with my sisters. That room had been used for lodgers, single
working men from Ireland, though more recently had been lived in
by his friend Mr. Doran, son of my grandparents' neighbors from
Ireland, with his wife Nellie and their young children. My mother
and Patricia had made it tidy for me and had gone to Woolworths to
buy a pillow and sheets and a coverlet for my bed. The room had a
fireplace for my own coal fire. I thought that finally my father had
come to an accommodation with me. That wasn't to be so but on
that night I felt safer than I could have imagined, as my parents
went out to the pub, and Patricia and I sat in my own room
excitedly going through the Stockton-Billingham Technical College
syllabus and the bus schedules I had been given, planning my
future.

Listening and dancing to Radio Luxembourg that evening had
a special sensation for me, as though the worst was over. I loved
my sister more I think than most boys love a sister. We were very
close and shared everything and I wanted to share my new world
with her but realized she too would have to forge her own way,
belittled by my father yelling at her often that education was no
good for a girl, that she'd just get married and have children,
cursing and hitting at her. That thought made me feel helpless,
wanting so much to encourage her to keep reading and learning so
finally we would both escape. I knew we were equally intelligent,
talking of many things we wondered about the world around us, but
I was a year older and she hadn't got the same opportunities I'd had
and she still did not have her own room.

Patricia had been taken to Ballybohan when she was eight,
after I was taken away to Derby Street, and had two years of
freedom, learning in the Sacred Heart convent school, and still
could say her prayers in Irish, so it kept us close together speaking

62

Survivor

small amounts of Irish secretly together even though I was losing much of what I had known. On returning to Derby Street she was enrolled in a convent school on Norton Road where the nuns taught her to be a proper young lady and was among a selected group of girls chosen to study for the Northern Counties Examinations in which the previous June she had passed all her examinations. Being a girl and that being the times her schedule of studies were not the same as mine. She passed in English, English Literature, Mathematics, History, Religious Knowledge, Shorthand, Typing, and Cookery. She gained a distinction in Typing and a Credit in Mathematics. That achievement carried no encouragement from our father, forcing her to get a job barely two weeks past her fifteenth birthday. Undaunted by that she had continued studying three nights a week at the Stockton-Billingham Technical College in Stockton. She was positive about what I would be able to do going to night school, sharing a common belief we had of looking for a silver lining in the darkest cloud. Prior to that time she had jobs like I had, with a baby-sitting job and working in a small shop selling bits and pieces for two hours after school. When she was fourteen she got a job each Saturday working on a stall in the North Ormsby market, on the south part of Middlesbrough. It was a long bus ride for her to get there by eight in the morning, working throughout the day until getting back to Derby Street by six in the evening with the enormous sum of ten shillings and sixpence, encountering our father with his hand out, demanding most of that money, threatening and cursing to enforce his demand.

Patricia and I had ways to save at least some of our money but it wasn't much so we had developed a way to pool our coins so that each week one of us could get a luxury item. The first week we did it we went down to look in the windows of the Co-operative clothing store. Patricia was looking at a handbag in one window while I was looking at a golden brown sweater in another window. Patricia had never had a handbag and I'd never had a sweater. As I looked over at my sister and saw her hope and happiness that we had this plan my feelings of love for her caught at my heart and I quickly said: "you go first". She hadn't expected that. In the social climate of the times the boy always went first, the girl was only

63

Survivor

secondary. So on that day Patricia got her handbag, and the next week I got my golden brown sweater. Three little words that meant so much to my sister, less to me since I was not even aware of the gender oppression around me, so imbued as I was with the times and the society I lived in. There were many other times like that afterwards but that first day was very special and in different ways influenced our thinking in later years.

So on my first day in I.C.I. we were both employed in full time jobs. I was a laboratory assistant and Patricia was an office junior. She had been very unhappy in her first office junior job but that lasted only ten weeks until she met a former teacher who got her a much better office junior job in which she was much happier and appreciated by her employer who encouraged her to keep striving, building up her confidence for the future, working for the next two years there while I worked in I.C.I., both of us going to night school.

In these early months of 1961 there was light ahead for Patricia. As she reached her sixteenth birthday she met a friend, a young man older than us, two years older than me, at a Catholic Youth club. Billy Taylor was tall and strong, muscular from working as a bricklayer's apprentice, with a ready smile and an easy laugh, confident from living life with loving parents in a respectable home. At nineteen he still was not yet a match for the violence of my father but he took many of the blows aimed at my sister. He didn't go away, he held my sister's hand walking down the street, he quietly and unknown to anyone, not even my sister, began to take karate lessons.

64

Survivor

Chapter 5

The early weeks of working for Mr. Rudd went by with new things to learn every day. I adjusted quickly to wearing my knee length white lab coat, wearing eyeglasses with safety glass, washing my hands frequently and drying them on the white paper towels mounted at the ends of the laboratory benches.

I took his advice seriously to never touch my face or eyes when working; a habit I was told would avoid the possibility of transferring a dangerous or toxic substance to my face.

I'd enrolled at Stockton-Billingham Technical College and opened my bank account. I was thrilled and excited to take the minibus down to the medical center at the very center of the factory complex, a couple of miles looking out the window at immense metal buildings, pipes of different colors everywhere along the side of the road and overhead, marveling at large billboards at frequent intervals, black print on white, declaring 'Last accident 67 days', 'Last accident 231 days', and so many other days since the last accident, the bus driver telling us that the company wanted even minor accidents to be reported.

A couple of weeks after starting work I returned to within the factory for a day of safety training. I learned how to operate the various kinds of fire extinguishers in use and how to use several kinds of gas masks and in the afternoon, heart pounding and ready, stood in line with my fellow trainees awaiting my turn to enter a hundred foot tunnel above ground that was filled with ammonia gas. Each of us were expected to check our goggles were a good fit and hold our breath as the door was opened for us to enter, not panic, locate a gas mask hanging on the wall, put it on, tighten it, then walk slowly through the tunnel to the end and back out again. When that was done I felt obscurely proud that I and the other eight trainees had not been driven to panic and run for the door at the end of the tunnel. The men teaching us explained that much of what we had learned was not likely to be used in the laboratory buildings since older and more experienced people would be around. However if any of us were to be assigned work in the factory it

65

Survivor

would require several days of more safety training even if we were to be working there for only a few weeks.

There were open covered bike sheds next to 'O' Building and on days it did not rain I rode my bike to work and to school. I enjoyed that, cycling to work, saving the bus fare, taking less time than the bus, immensely proud that I was earning a real wage, then correcting my thoughts to salary, planning what I was going to do when the money arrived in my bank account. I'd already bought two new white shirts and two long grey trousers from the Co-operative clothing store before starting work but more clothes would have to wait until I got paid.

Up to that point my mother had taken the family laundry to a launderette on Norton Road but in the flush of working an important regular job I got the idea of asking Mary to wash my clothes separately once a week. I told her I'd give her sixpence each time as well as the money for the machine and washing powder as well as sixpence to share with Tom and Terry if she took them with her to watch the washing machine and drier. There was a candy shop next to the launderette and for Mary and my brothers it was a voyage and a respite away from Derby Street for several hours. Mary's eagerness to do it and the wide smile and glistening happy eyes as I handed her the money and my pillow sack of laundry along with the responsibility that I was giving to her has been with me all my life and given me happiness whenever I've reflected about her willingness to help me, always ready to remind me that it was time to get my clothes washed. She would fold the clothes neatly but I would iron them. That involved heating a cast iron on the gas stove, holding the top with a cloth, then putting a damp cloth on the shirts and trousers as I ironed, making sure I got a good crease on the trouser legs. I made sure my father was never around when I did that for I was sure he would mock me and tell me I was 'putting on airs'.

A great joy to me was the clean smelling white tiled toilets on the ground floor of 'O' Building with real toilet paper and rows of porcelain sinks with soap dispensers and hot and cold water. I'd cycle to work a half hour early to luxuriate in not having to use the fetid toilet at home. I'd developed an urge to be as clean as

66

Survivor

possible, an anxiety troubling me that I was getting acne on my face and chest and back, some of the pimples turning septic. I was afraid of the next step I was going to take but I was convinced the dirt and lack of proper washing in Derby Street was the cause of my acne. I knew that in town next to the swimming baths, near to the central police station, was a building called the 'Turkish Baths' where men could get a bath. I had an obscure feeling that disreputable men would go there, perverts, men my father called 'poofters', men who would frighten me, but my cystic acne and fear it would get much worse drove me to grit my teeth and one day I walked in the door. It wasn't at all what I had feared. There were two old men taking the money and handing out two big white towels with soap and taking me to a private bathroom, with a door to lock behind me, one of many along a corridor, telling we to take as long as I wanted, and for the first time in my life I filled a freshly cleaned bath tub with hot and cold water, adjusting the taps to the right temperature, and felt my anxiety fade away as I scrubbed and cleaned myself, pleased I'd conquered my fear, determined I'd do this at least once a week. It wasn't expensive and I still had enough money saved to last me until I was paid, keeping my daily expenses on a folded piece of paper I kept in my pocket.

The I.C.I. cafeteria became a regular part of my life for my working days, two delicious full hot meals a day, learning to call them lunch and dinner, buying cheap sandwiches on my day release day. There was a small public library across the road from Stockton-Billingham Technical College and I made a friend there to have lunch with. Marjorie Naisbitt recognized me as soon as I walked in to look around. She was about my age and lived on Patterdale Avenue with her parents just across from my aunt Josie and her family. Marjorie was a junior librarian and had ambitions and an infectious laugh. I liked her immediately and she knew all about my father and family life so there was no need to pretend different and so we became great friends for many years afterward.

I made friends with my fellow day release classmates though not as close as with Marjorie, thinking there was a divide between us, with some of them clearly being of middle class. We did get along well together and after a few months began to meet after class

67

Survivor

in a hotel bar just across from the Empire cinema where my mother cleaned floors. They were a year older than me and were legal to drink beer. I would drink pints of crushed orange juice and we would play darts and have a good time with lots of laughter and joking. Stephen and Gary and Terry Cox were all from the city of York, forty eight miles south, and hadn't done well enough in their 'A' levels to get into university so had come to I.C.I. to repeat the exams. Terry had a racing bike like me and so we cycled to Stockton from school as the others got the bus. We were always first at the bar. I was in awe of Stephen. He was my height and handsome with a clear complexion and a friendly smile, wearing beautiful clothes and always smelled freshly clean and from the way he talked obviously came from some sort of upper class family.

None of us talked about our families so I soon became comfortable playing darts and having a good time with them.

I was able to spend as little time in Derby Street as possible when my father was likely to be around and so the end of January came with relatively few encounters between us and even then there was no more talk of me digging ditches and on a few occasions he even called me John. At that time he was going through one of his periods of work. He had the ability to drive an asphalt road laying machine with 16 gears, called a Barber-Greene. The foreman would come to the house early in the morning with a large metal canteen of beer to persuade my father to go to work. Years later Billy Taylor was to say that my father could have made something of himself if he wasn't drunk all the time, he had so many abilities and knew how to do lots of jobs in the building trades.

At work Mr. Rudd gave me increasing responsibilities in weighing samples, dissolving them in aqua-regia, diluting the cooled solutions, then accurately using a pipette to transfer sample solutions to volumetric flasks, adding a different complexing agent solution to each and then diluting to the volumetric mark. The range of different colors that produced gave me a sense of accomplishment. Mr. Rudd then would have me assist him measure the color intensity in small cells in an instrument called a Unicam Spectrometer. He continually and gently stressed that precision and

Survivor

accuracy and good record keeping every single time was important and if I was consistent on that I would get to go on to other jobs. He taught me that if I had an accident and dropped a flask then let it fall and jump back. "Let it fall", he said, "don't try to catch it. You could hurt yourself. Let it break. We'll clean it up. The sample can always be redone." I was very careful. I never dropped a flask. I wanted so much to please him and see him smile at me as I worked.

Near the end of January I was given a small brown envelope with a glassine window with my name and National Insurance Number YA 94 57 54 D. My hands were trembling. Mr. Rudd tapped me on the shoulder and motioned with his head to a corner of the laboratory. With a broad smile he said quietly: "go over there and sit down and come back when you are ready." I would have done anything for him. When I opened the envelope it was there right in front of me. I had to blink the tears from my eyes. I'd earned a salary for that month of twenty three pounds and fifteen shillings with deductions of two pounds and two shillings, almost equally divided between income tax and my National Insurance stamp, with twenty one pounds and eighteen shillings already deposited in my bank account that very day. I still had almost a pound left from my savings. I was filled with a sense of wonder and gratitude and determination. I could now do what I had planned all month.

I didn't go to the bank that day. I waited a couple of days until Friday. The couple of days were overcast with a light intermittent rain but I didn't want to get the bus. I cycled with my light yellow plastic rain Mac with hood that I'd used on my paper round. I didn't care. I enjoyed it. My plans were made. Friday lunch time I went and drew eleven pounds from the bank then cycled home bursting to tell my mother what I intended to do but knew I could not. She went with my father to the pub that night and I spent a restless night waiting for morning. I knew my father would be sleeping when my mother left to clean the cinema floors that Saturday and I told her I'd meet her as she finished work. She was usually finished by eleven o'clock but I was there by ten and waited for her. The women who worked with her were teasing me, trying to find out why I was there, was there trouble again with my Dad, what a big

69

lad I was getting, come on now give me a kiss, but I was non-committal, not wanting to share what I was going to do. When we left the Empire cinema, walking the length of the High Street, me pushing my bike, my mother reassured there wasn't trouble in Derby Street, I waited until we reached almost the end of Wellington Street and took her hand and turned right across the High Street toward the rent office. We were four weeks behind on the rent. I paid all four weeks and a week ahead. My mother began to cry, laughing at the same time. I took her then back across the High Street to Marks and Spenser's and bought a steam iron with an electric cord to attach to a socket, two new white shirts and two ties and a cheap pair of leather shoes, put ten shillings back into my pocket for the coming week, and gave her the rest. On the way back down Wellington Street to Derby Street she stopped to buy a chicken and some potatoes and never stopped talking after I told her that each week I'd give her the rent and money for food for us all. I knew I'd easily be able to do that. I didn't need much. I knew how to be frugal and I'd still have money to buy more clothes. I just didn't want to let my father get any of it.

As we ate the roasted chicken and potatoes late that afternoon I was tense and afraid of my father. He had the look I'd first seen when he came to pick me up in Ballybohan, a frightening smile as if he intended to do me harm. He had taken the news that I'd paid the rent better than I'd expected, not raging at me or punching me, not even calling me you bastard. He'd got his wage packet the night before and had gone to the pub with it so he must still have money in his pocket.

After I went into my parlor room to study my chemistry notes from class he came in and told me I was to go with him to his favorite pub to meet his friends. I was stunned at that, not knowing what to think, bewildered at what seemed to be a different tactic in his relationship with me. I didn't argue, wanting to keep this relatively peaceful atmosphere going as long as possible. I thought I could weather the time of my father telling his drinking friends about my job without danger, remembering the Irishmen who had looked out for me in the fields where I had learned to hoe mangels from Martin, who had told my father to leave me alone. The pub

Survivor

was thick with cigarette smoke and beer fumes and a lot of working class men in rough clothes. I didn't see Martin and began to panic. I was sitting at a pub table with four men I didn't know as pints of beer were brought to the table by my father who then unexpectedly placed a pint of beer in front of me. At that time in England legal drinking age was eighteen and it would be four weeks until I would be seventeen but in that particular pub such things were ignored. I sat looking at the pint with a sinking feeling, seeing a future crashing into ruins in my mind, looking back up to the men around the table grinning at me and raising their pints in a salute to me, seeing with horror what my father's plan was, to make me a drunk like him, to spend all my money on him and his friends in the pubs, to marry and beat my children, to live forever in a place like Derby Street. A sudden impulse gripped me, wanting to flee from that place, and I took the pint of beer as if to sip from it then upended it spilling the amber beer all over the table and the floor, the pint glass upside down, and I ran as fast as I could out the door and down the street, hearing shouts and angers behind me.

I wandered the streets for hours, knowing I was going to get battered that night, seeing dismal days ahead, having nowhere to go, not regretting what I had done, determined that I was not going to walk on the road my father had planned for me. Finally I went back to Derby Street. Patricia was getting ready to go out with Billy. My mother had gone to join my father in the pub. Mary had my laundry neatly folded on my bed in the parlor room. I ironed my shirts and trousers with the new steam iron, marveling at the technology despite my grief, then took my clothes and shoes and socks and underwear in brown paper bags to hang from the handlebars of my bike and pushed my bike over to Grandmother Dobson and Aunt Jean's house on Mill Street West where I told them what I had done and pleaded with them to let me sleep there for just a few nights until my father wouldn't be so angry with me. They understood and praised me and Aunt Jean cooked a late night supper. I needed that after the events of the day. I knew I could endure a minor beating after a few days but didn't think I could survive a major beating from my father at the height of his drunken anger. I returned to Derby Street after work on Monday and was

Survivor

once again you bastard, enduring several punches and curses, but that was nothing to me, just as long as he didn't hit me in the face, exposing my shame to Mr. Rudd and the other people in the laboratory.

In the following weeks I did my studying in the front room of Mill Street West and in the public library, going back to Derby Street very late at night just to sleep, then rising early in the morning and going for an hour of cycle riding before going to work. I'd stopped going to confession a year before because I could not make an honest confession and now I stopped going to Mass. It seemed to me as if God had abandoned me. I had nobody to speak in Irish to, Patricia spending as much time as she could at night school and with Billy, and the cadences and phrases were fading from my mind. As I reached my seventeenth birthday at the beginning of March Mr. Rudd gave me a birthday card and had brought in a rich fruit cake with a candle on top for everyone in the laboratory to share. I was overwhelmed. I couldn't remember ever having a birthday cake. He then told me I had done well working for him and I was to be assigned my own job at the far end of the laboratory running what he called 'a carbon train'. I was to learn how to do it from the lad doing it for a week before he moved on to his next assignment. The lad was only twenty and had a strong rural accent from the Durham coal fields to the north of Stockton so I had to pay close attention to his instructions and the stress he placed on accuracy and the importance of the job. His accent reminded me of the way my cousin Earnest from Bishop Auckland spoke so I liked him right away. He told me the proper name was combustion train and it was called a carbon train because in that laboratory it was used only for carbon analysis. The samples were soot taken from various sites around I.C.I. and were expected to range from ninety seven percent to almost a hundred percent carbon and I was to learn how to calculate that to the first decimal space. He explained any lower that that meant there could be contamination from a leak in a reactor or a pipe and had to be reported immediately to the laboratory supervisor. It involved weighing a sample into a white clay 'boat', putting a strip of tin on top, placing it into near the center of a two foot horizontal pipe, connecting two

72

Survivor

glass U-tubes at one end of the pipe, the first containing dry calcium chloride to collect moisture, the second containing soda-lime to collect carbon dioxide. I had to pass dry nitrogen through the pipe with the U-tubes initially disconnected, flushing out any residual moisture, then quickly connect the U-tubes, begin heating beneath the boat with a Bunsen burner, next turning the regulator valves so dry air would flow through the cylinder. I was already confident in the accuracy of my weighing, and I soon became adept at using and reading the regulator valves at the top of the tall cylinders of dry nitrogen and dry air strapped to the side of the laboratory bench. Weighing the soda-lime U-tube before and after a run gave the weight of accumulated carbon dioxide and an easy calculation then gave the percentage of carbon in the original sample. The lad showed me how to empty, clean and repack the U-tubes after several runs when the dye level in the solid materials showed depletion of the capacity to absorb. He told me I could learn to do six or seven runs a day.

Within weeks I was doing eight runs a day on my full days and even matched that on my night school days when I left at 4:30 by arriving at 7:30 in the morning. There was a strict rule that nobody could work in the laboratory alone but usually there was at least one other person who arrived early so it worked for me. I kept good and neat notes in my laboratory book and transferred them to official forms every day before leaving. I knew Mr. Rudd was watching me and sometimes would come over to talk to me and that would make me feel proud and important.

My life developed into a routine of work and classes and cycling and avoiding confrontations with my father, giving my mother money for the rent and food Saturday morning, after my father had spent his money in the pubs Friday night. It seemed to work. Each month I bought some more clothes and I got an urge to buy myself a suit. I only had a vague idea what a suit would do for me but I'd go look in the windows of a men's clothing store called Alexander's near the end of the High Street. It was a store for the upper class people because all the suits on display were priced in guineas, that being an upper class way of expressing prices, but I knew that a guinea was actually one pound and one shilling and I

Survivor

didn't let that intimidate me. I had begun saving my money for that day but each week would go look in the windows.

There was one time when Patricia borrowed my precious golden brown sweater to go to a dance with Billy and it caused the only ever flare up between us when she gave it back with the smell of perfume on it. I was upset, thinking of what the other lads I knew would think of me, smelling the perfume on me, adding to the uneasy feelings I had about myself, feelings I couldn't even share with Patricia, reasons that had caused me to stop going to confession.

As the eldest of the five of us I felt a strong identity with my sisters and brothers, thinking of us as the grandchildren of Bridget Fahey in Ballybohan, submerging my father into the background, wanting so much that he would go away and leave us in peace. I was happy that Patricia now had Billy by her side and felt a sense of relief that she now had a boyfriend who was doing his best to protect her. Mary would concern me at times. I'd read up on scarlet fever in the medical books at Stockton Public Library and it chilled me when I read that scarlet fever carried later complications of heart disease and rheumatic fever. It was now long past but I couldn't get out of my mind being told by our parents that she was going to die when she was taken away to the isolation hospital. She was thin and healthy looking with pink cheeks but she was clearly not growing much, would not become as tall as Patricia and me, was always so very quiet and reserved and would run and hide whenever my father would erupt into drunken rages, battering at me and my mother., breaking furniture, smashing plates and cups, shouting and cursing and demanding we sing rebel songs.

Up to that point I'd thought of Tommy and Terry as babies but that changed when one day it came out that my little brothers were enterprising. Tommy was seven and Terry was six and they had become friends with an eight year old boy called Dennis Squires. Dennis had a father who was a window cleaner and they lived near us on one of the better houses on Wellington Street. The father had made them small ladders and given them small buckets and window cleaning materials and Dennis and Tommy and Terry were building up a business on the local streets, knocking on doors

74

Survivor

and offering to clean ground floor windows, collecting sixpences and sometimes shillings for their work. It lasted for less than a month until the Police came and told them to stop, it was against some law, but it did bring a reporter to Derby Street and the three of them got an article and pictures in the Evening Gazette. So at so young an age my little brothers comforted me that they too had the urge to survive and succeed, that they wouldn't let our family life grind them down.

After several months of working on the carbon train I was assigned my next job. It was analyzing moisture content in fertilizers made in the factory. The supervisor of the laboratory sat me down and explained that accuracy was very important. He said to me that if a thousand tons of fertilizer was shipped to a country like Libya with a manifest saying it was 3.5% moisture and the chemists in Libya determined it was more than that when it arrived, even by a small amount, they could refuse to pay for it and it would be too expensive for I.C.I. to ship it back and I.C.I. would lose a lot of money. I'd already been praised by Mr. Rudd and the lad who had taught me to run the carbon train so I was confident I could tackle this next task and it thrilled me when he told me that these type of assignments would only last for about three months, learning from the person doing the job each time, so that we would all get a range of experience.

I was doing well in my classes at Stockton-Billingham Technical College, learning more chemistry all the time, as well as physics and mathematics, I was growing taller and hungry all the time, still in dismay at the spread of my acne but keeping myself as clean as possible and had become a regular at the Turkish Baths.

I could imagine that very many young people of the age I was then have a blessing upon them that comes from not knowing what is ahead, living daily triumphs despite angers and setbacks and frustrations to be tackled on a daily basis. So it was for me, not knowing or thinking of even greater trials yet to come, feeling I had my life under control, innocent that I endured the punches and curses from my father as though they were of less consequence than my other life at work and classes. It seemed as if it had baffled my father that my salary was deposited into a bank in Billingham and

Survivor

was completely under my control. Sadly that wasn't so for Patricia who had to go back to Derby Street each week with money in a pay packet, vulnerable to his threats and demands. I always made sure I'd only have less than ten shillings in coins in my pocket as I'd wheel my bike into the hallway beside the parlor room. I'd cycle to Billingham Saturday mornings to get the money to give my mother. It was much more difficult for Patricia and I knew that Billy was buying her what she needed after our father would give her little back from her pay packet. That seemed to me to be very unfair and not right. So if he grabbed at me and went through my pockets he'd find only coins and I'd shrug off the blows and curses as if it was some sort of tribute. So was my life then and if it hardened me I didn't know it.

The new job I had of analyzing moisture content in fertilizers only took me three days to become totally able to use the instrument. I learned to titrate the deep brown Karl Fischer reagent into a swirling methanol and fertilizer glass vessel, the spinning magnetic bar at the bottom of the vessel fascinating me as I made sure it was special dry methanol I used. The instrument and vessel was protected from external moisture with nitrogen, the end point coming when the Karl Fisher reagent had all been reacted with the moisture and a tinge of brown appeared. It was a powerful feeling for me doing a good job, my total attention in focus on the titration, wanting always to be the best at the task, hungry for the praise of Mr. Rudd and my laboratory supervisor, filling out the official forms of the record of my day's work before leaving for the day. I set myself objectives to complete each day even if it meant staying longer on days I didn't have night school. I didn't get any extra money for that since I was on salary but that didn't matter to me. I'd like to stay until the older workers in the laboratory were finishing up for the day and the platinum vessels were being locked up in a safe for the night. Mr. Rudd used to tease me and say: "come on John. That's it for the day. We don't want to have to send for your dinner."

Much later on I was amazed to find out it wasn't actually a joke, that at times of crisis when work urgently needed to be done a call from the laboratory supervisor that his assistants were working

Survivor

more than an hour over regular hours would soon bring the clatter of a trolley coming down the hallway laden with covered plates of hot food, pushed by a woman from the cafeteria.

Marjorie Naisbitt had begun to join us in our darts sessions in the bar below the hotel, down stairs at the outside of the hotel, almost as though going below ground. She was popular with my classmates and they began referring to her as my girlfriend. That made me feel as though I belonged, was doing the sort of thing other lads did though in truth I had feelings toward her no more than a warm and happy friendship. After a while she stopped coming after one evening a girl just a little older than I turned up. Her name was Diana and she seemed to take a special liking for me.

Diana had come down from a room on the upper part of the hotel called a 'cocktail bar'. I had never ventured there and wasn't even sure of what a 'cocktail' was, imagining it to be a mix of a strong drink like whiskey with fruit juice, favored by upper class young men and women, dressed in expensive elegant clothing, chatting in vowel swallowing accents about topics that would be mysteries to me. Diana was very beautiful, several inches shorter than me, slender, with long blond hair and blue eyes, a clear fresh complexion, perfectly groomed, clothes that were surely bought in some distant place far from us working classes. She enchanted me, sitting close to her on a wooden bench as I took my breaks during the dart games. She had a delicate hint of perfume that she told me was a special blend from Paris and talked of trips to London and foreign places. In the following weeks I found out that she was almost the same age as me, lived with her parents near Yarm, and had her own horse in a field behind her home. It all seemed so exotic to me. When closing time came at half past ten we got into a custom of walking up and down the High Street, our arms encircling each other, stopping in secluded shop doorways to kiss. At that time of the night the streets would be emptying, all the shops closed much earlier, streetlights illuminating our wandering. At times we would be told to move on from a shop doorway by a policeman, but not unkindly, more a sort of amused caution. When I would put my arms around and embrace Diana, feeling the warmth of her body, smelling her perfume, talking and kissing, I'd

Survivor

feel the tensions and fears of my life retreat from me, wanting for those feelings to go on forever. At times I would get an erection, knowing she would be aware of it through our clothing, but it just seemed natural and we didn't talk of it. I'd long since relieved those tensions in the traditional way known to young men, the way in which the priests told us would make us blind, us not believing it and ignoring it, and had surges of emotion, being of a healthy vigor and, as they say, red-blooded. But in the months we walked the High Street until each time she had to get the last bus home to Yarm, I never went further, thoughts of pregnancy and whether I carried my father's trait of beating his children intruding at the last minute.

In the following months I began to think a lot about myself, admitting to myself that the feelings I had with Diana, wanting the warmth of close bodily contact in an embrace with someone who loved me, who I cared for, talking and kissing, sharing dreams, feeling the anxieties and troubles of my life retreat to a distant place, wanting a brighter future, was something I'd long wanted with another lad my own age, good looking like I thought of myself, despite the acne. Not that I'd ever met such a lad, banishing such thoughts as they came to me, thinking I was the only one, thinking it was a sin.

A day came when I walked into Stockton Public Library on Wellington Street and went to the psychology shelf that I had been avoiding. I found and began to read a book by Kraft Ebbing, a noted authority, and was devastated by what I was reading. According to him I had a sexual perversion called homosexuality and I was doomed to become a horrible person, a terrible person, someone I would despise. Adjacent books gave me the same story and I discovered that according to the laws of England if I ever even tried to find another lad to love me we would be judged criminals and put into jail.

After a few hours I left those books behind me and walked out onto Wellington Street in despair. I got on my bike and cycled to St. Mary's Church on Norton Road where I had been an altar boy. There was nobody there at that time of the day and I was able to kneel in a pew at the back of the Church and cry. I prayed and

78

Survivor

pleaded with God to take my life before such a calamity would come upon me. I knew to take my own life would be a grave mortal sin but God in his mercy could take my life and save me. Please God, I prayed, I've accepted being a bastard, being beaten by my father, unable to protect my mother and my sisters and brothers, being taken out of school, having acne, but this is just too much a burden, that I could be judged a criminal and put into jail. Please God, take my life, I have tried to be a good person, I am still pure, and I have avoided sin.

Diana and I drifted apart. I stopped going to darts sessions for a while, thinking my classmates would see something in my eyes that would reveal me, cycling for hours each day with despair gripping me, tearing at my heart, not able to talk with anyone about the disaster I saw ahead of me. My acne was getting worse and in some way I felt that was a judgment upon me. So went several months as my classes ended for that term and I plunged myself into my laboratory work, proving to myself I was good for something. I found out that Stockton-Billingham Technical College had summer evening classes that were condensed into a day release day, four evenings and Saturday morning. I went to the nice personnel man to ask if I could do that and he assured me that I could. Somehow he knew that I went in early on my days for evening classes and I flushed and was embarrassed when he teased me about it, assuring himself that I would still go to dinner in the cafeteria before going to class, telling me that Mr. Rudd was proud of me. So in that way I sought knowledge of chemistry, physics, and mathematics as the way to sustain me through months of unhappiness and despair.

As a result of my determination I decided to take 'O' level examinations in Additional Pure Mathematics and Applied Mathematics being set by the University of London. Within weeks I found that I had passed. So along with my eight passes from the Joint Matriculation Board set by the Universities of Manchester, Liverpool, Leeds, Sheffield, and Birmingham, the northern universities, I now had ten 'O' levels, with my University of London passes in mathematics added to my earlier Mathematics Syllabus I from the Joint Matriculation Board; meaning I now had three passes in mathematics. It soothed my spirit, proving I was at

79

least good for something, resistance in me that I was setting up a bulwark against thoughts that would lead me into sin, would make me a criminal.

At the beginning of the summer my Laboratory supervisor and Mr. Rudd took me to lunch and told me I was to be recommended for a position as Laboratory Assistant in the Standardisation Laboratory on the ground floor of 'O' Building, nearer to the front entrance. It would be an important permanent job but there would be several candidates and it would be dependent on eye tests I was to take because it was important to have good color vision across the red/yellow and blue/green parts of the spectrum. I knew I had good eyesight and was optimistic I could pass the tests. The next day I went to the optical office, near to 'O' Building, next to the I.C.I. library, and was tested. I had to turn pages in a couple of large books covered in dots of different colors and sizes and tell the woman watching me what number or letter I saw on each page. It seemed easy to me, only faltering near the end of each book, and the woman seemed pleased with me. I won the position and after a week of showing another lad how to run the Karl Fischer apparatus I began work in the Standardisation Laboratory, a position I was going to hold until going to University.

I've reflected often in my life about my good fortune in the Marist priests at St. Mary's College getting me a job working in Billingham for Imperial Chemical Industries. Although the company had other industrial sites in England ours was the main location. I worked for the Agricultural Division and the other was the Heavy Organic Chemical Division; heavy in the sense of multi tonnage production. Actually in my eyes at the time it was an astonishing enormous production of fertilizers and other materials. During my trip to the medical center in the center of the factory, the original farmhouse set in lawns, a square of land surrounded on all sides with reactors and roads and pipes, open sky overhead, the driver of the minibus took us by a huge building open to the road where we could see a pile of granular fertilizer surely well over a hundred feet tall and chuckled when he told us the story of early days when it was found there was a critical mass for the pile when it exploded and spread fertilizer all over Tees-side, alarming many

Survivor

but welcomed by many gardeners, it being enough to enrich gardens for several years afterward. He pointed out the roof was on hydraulic supports that would lift if another explosion happened then laughed out loud and said in his broad Durham accent: "not that we'd want that to happen again, would we lads", establishing that as an old man he was a long time worker in the factory. There was a loyalty to the company that I've not found matched by any company I've worked for since. Then again I've not worked for any company with the range of benefits given to all of us. The annual bonus of voting shares based on profit applied to everyone, salaried workers and all wage earners alike. In the manufacturing plant workers were encouraged to write in suggestions for improvements from which they would be given an additional bonus if it saved money for the company. In the years while I was there one time a man suggested that the trains bringing in coal would be more efficient if the coal was unloaded at one end of the site than the other. I think even he must have been surprised when it was done and after six months, calculations gave him the money saved in that six months, that being the policy, amounting to several years wages. The company had a long article on him in the company glossy magazine with pictures of him and his wife at a congratulatory dinner as they were given an additional bonus of a world cruise. The man was near retirement and must surely have been overwhelmed by his success from such a simple observation.

The basis of fertilizer production was the ammonia works, combining nitrogen from the air and hydrogen from the synthetic fuels plant, that being produced from coal coming from the Durham coal mines to the north, with catalysts and water and pressure and heat. There was a sulphuric acid plant in which suphur was oxidized to sulphur dioxide which was added to air and oxidized further to sulphur trioxide which on combination with water gave sulphuric acid. Raw materials for the sulphuric acid plant and fertilizers were mined from anhydrite, calcium sulphate, brought up from tunnels and caverns in the ground below. The sulphuric acid plant was the origin of an amusing story that caused much laughter when told in the pubs at night. The company policy was that any discarded equipment or supplies in the factory complex could be

Survivor

taken home by any worker on filling out a form to be shown to the guards at the factory gate when leaving for the day. The catalyst pipe for oxidizing suphur dioxide to sulphur trioxide used large grids of platinum wire for the catalysis. Every so often the grids had to be replaced due to damage of the surface of the wire. Platinum was very expensive and the grids would be cleaned and recovered. One day the damaged platinum wire grids lying at the side of the pipe went missing. There was a great uproar, it was a major event, platinum theft, investigations and police and talk of criminals went on for months. Until one day a man was admiring his neighbor's garden a few hundred yards from the main gate and saw the shiny metal 'chicken wire' his neighbor had erected to keep in a few hens. It was all quite innocent. His neighbor was a worker in the factory, saw the grids lying there, and in thinking they were discarded, picked them up, filled out the form, walked out the factory gate, felt he had got some very nice 'chicken wire'. How was he to know, he was only a laborer in the factory, he was a loyal employee, he knew the company was good to the workers. After the platinum grids were recovered and the excitement died down the man didn't even lose his job. He'd revealed a fault in the discarded equipment procedure. He didn't get a bonus for that though.

The day-release program on full pay was available to all young employees. At Stockton-Billingham Technical College there were classrooms for welding and pipe fitting and plumbing and electrical work. Other parts of the building were for typing and shorthand and office skills, all those other day-release students getting ready for their own examinations, building skills, for the benefit of not just my company but other companies in the area. It wasn't at all unusual for us studying for our 'A' levels in chemistry, physics and mathematics to be in classrooms next to others learning welding and pipe fitting and all those other skills, meeting each other in the corridors and the College cafeteria, laughing and joking together, not thinking of any division between us, we were all working class, we were learning. If some few of us came from middle class families it was not mentioned, not part of our lives.

Those of us from my company used to refer to ourselves as 'ici people', pronounced with a hard firm c, proud of our nickname,

82

loyal to our company. We all had been told that our service with the company would always be on record and if we went on into life to work for other companies we could always return with our years of service restored to us and counted toward future benefits. We were told that if we managed to get into university we would be given leave of absence with the company paying for our National Insurance stamps while we were gone, expected to return during summer holidays, to be given a salary that we would have got if we had stayed working and not gone to university. It was a solid invigorating feeling to belong, to know that Imperial Chemical Industries was looking out for me, was security for me, and would always be there for me.

So as the months of warm weather came in I was able to occupy my thoughts and time with work and classes, trying not to think of the horrible things I'd read in the psychology books, still reading used paperback science fiction books and magazines from Stockton market, taking out novels from the Wellington Street library, reading with a hunger to know more, to find a way to escape, going back to Derby Street very late at night, just to sleep. I'd got to the point of reading a novel in one or two hours, my classes seemed so logical and easy for me, the violence and angers of my father were something I just endured, making sure that every Saturday morning after class I cycled fast to my bank to get my mother money for the rent and food.

I learned a great deal more about the importance of precision and accuracy in the Standardisation Laboratory. The head of the laboratory was Mr. Redman, an elderly large heavyset man with a gruff exterior, intimidating to me at first until I became accustomed to his high standards and until I realized he was very territorial toward anyone entering the laboratory, even those nominally his superiors, but fiercely protective of his assistants. He had been with I.C.I. since he was young and had been on a team doing very secret research on producing uranium hexafluoride during World War Two. He had built up the Standardisation Laboratory over many years and still had a glass container containing a large quantity of yellow uranium oxide, depleted of its radioactive isotope, on a shelf. The laboratory had a temperature control system maintaining

Survivor

a temperature of 68 degrees Fahrenheit, that being the temperature at which he had standardized the titration burettes. He got the burettes from the National Bureau of Standards, long narrow burettes that could contain 100 ml of solution. They had a thistle reservoir at the top with a meniscus mark in the neck of the thistle, and the long slender graduated body for the last 15 ml, finely graduated, a white square of ceramic clipped to top and bottom to get accurate meniscus readings. He restandardised those burettes himself, rejecting those not within his high standards. The titrations were done in a white tiled fume cupboard with brilliant non-flicker lighting, with stools at the bench so two laboratory assistants could work side by side. The job was to make various molar and tenth molar solutions of hydrochloric acid and sodium hydroxide in sixty liter rigid polystyrene carboys and standardize them to a high degree of accuracy each day. I was trained to do reproducible titrations with accuracy of 100.00 ml +/- 0.02 ml, learning how to watch for the first sign of the indicator phenolphthalein tinge appearing, swirling the beaker smoothly with a wrist action, knowing when to tip the end of the burette to the side of the flask for the last fraction of a drop. I was trained by a man called Dave Nicholson, who had been in the army, and was good natured and friendly, patient with me as I learned the techniques. There was also another lad about five years older than me, from a colliery village to the north. I regret I've forgotten his name. He was very helpful in teaching me everything he knew, laughing and joking as he talked to me. There were other standard solutions made there, sodium thiosulphate and ceric sulphate and sometimes a special order, using different indicators, which is why I'd had the eye tests, learning to get to a precise titration end point. We would transfer the solutions each day to 2.5 liter amber glass Winchesters according to order forms from various parts of I.C.I., to be sent out each morning. I can still smile when thinking of Mr. Redman bellowing at some unfortunate person coming to us with a request that didn't follow procedure; "this is a service...not a shop.." he'd yell at the top of his voice, sending the unfortunate scurrying back out into the corridor. He would brook no interference with us as we worked.

84

Survivor

I met many other people when I worked there, becoming comfortable and confident with my status. In the early part of August I met two older men, Roger and Clive, who invited me to join them one weekend to walk the Lyke Wake walk. It opened my mind to more of the world and broadened my horizons. It was my first adventure. It instilled in me the belief that every young person, especially those in the kind of circumstances I was living in, should have the opportunity to achieve a physical endurance trek under the open sky, away from the horror and angers of surviving violence and drunkenness, being reliant and trusting guidance from kind and responsible adults. The horrors and angers can be subdued and left behind for the adventure. I found that with Roger and Clive. I had assured them that I could walk the forty miles across the north Yorkshire moors, that my legs were strong from cycle riding, that I could keep up, that I was eager to go with them, that I wouldn't let them down. They told me to wear old shoes with woolen socks, with more socks and changes of clothing, a sweater for the colder stretches, and a plastic Mac in case of rain. They would have the ordnance survey maps, a compass, the Lyke Wake guide, sandwiches and lemonade. I bought a small used backpack from the Army and Navy store and I was ready, standing at the end of Wellington Street by seven o'clock that Saturday evening. It was market day and the High Street was thronged with shoppers, a clear sky with high drifting clouds, hours yet until it would get dark, excited and hoping that I wasn't dreaming, thrilled when Clive's friend pulled up in front of me, in a car, right on time, welcoming me, taking me away from the pubs and the fears, bringing me to happiness for a while.

Clive's friend would drive us to the start point in Osmotherly, a small hamlet nineteen miles south of Stockton, and would pick us up twenty four hours later in Ravenscar on the coast. As we headed out of the High Street, along Yarm road, on to Yarm and across the river Tees there, south to Osmotherly through countryside that expanded my anticipations, Roger sat with me on the back seat and explained what we were about to do, showing me the route on an ordnance survey map, telling me about the tradition of the 'Crossing' as it was called. The objective was to complete the forty

85

Survivor

mile crossing in less than twenty four hours to become members of the Lyke Wake club. Roger had done it before. It was Clive's first time. Roger was in charge of showing us how to register at a 'trig' marker near a pub in Osmotherly, guiding us across, and then registering at a 'trig' point near a house in Ravenscar on the coast. The Lyke wake crossing is a walk across the north Yorkshire moors, desolate and covered in heather and bracken, crossing some country roads in places, walking on an old overgrown Roman road at one point, passing near the Fylingdales early warning radar station at another. We could choose our own route since there wasn't a defined track, walking through the heather, just making sure we would pass through the highest points. Some of those points were 'trig' points, concrete markers, at up to three thousand feet above sea level at the highest, the ordnance survey map filled with strange and exotic names given to places from ancient times, places we would pass through, defining separate moors and bogs and ravines, for in the lower sections we would have to be careful not to walk into a bog or fall into a ravine. Roger had told us we would walk the first couple of hours while were still fresh, and after sunset could still walk further until resting for a few hours under the stars. At that time of the year it never gets really dark and with a half moon riding in the sky, stray high drifting clouds, a multitude of stars, good comradeship, the scent of the blooming heather, I had a feeling of happiness and achievement that spread out into gratitude that Roger and Clive had including me on their crossing.

As an early dawn lightened the sky I was enthralled by the land around me. Other people had described it as bleak and desolate. I didn't see it that way at all. To me it was magnificent, seeing for miles across the heather, the bees and pollinating insects busy at their work, with us far from other people, the open sky and the calls of birds bringing me the freedom that comes with being one with nature. I realized as I walked that I was going through another part of growing up, an experience that would strengthen me and give me hope I could tackle any problem in my future. Later on Sunday, as we descended from the higher points, we walked for a short time on an old overgrown Roman road. Roger was delighted that he had managed to locate it for me. He knew of how excited

86

Survivor

I'd been of that prospect; of walking on the stones laid down during the Roman occupation of England, linking me to the past, solidifying my identity to history and long ago. After that we stood amid the heather and bracken looking down onto lower ground a few miles away where we could see the huge white 'golf balls' of the Fylingdales Early Warning Radar Station. Huge in the sense they were massive, needing a better description than golf ball. That point brought me to an awareness of the immensity of the world, with the past on the Roman road behind me, the future in the Radar Station, my resolution to succeed becoming stronger on seeing the North Sea in the distance as we descended into Ravenscar. We made it, coming in under twenty four hours. I was a member of the Lyke Wake club as soon as I signed my name and time in the log book at the house in Ravenscar. I only had a couple of blisters and that didn't bother me and when they dropped me off at the end of Wellington Street late that evening I felt as if I had been gone for weeks.

During the following week going to work and night school I had a constant glow of achievement burning within me until one evening disaster came upon me. I was cycling to Stockton-Billingham College on my day release day when I was hit by a car. It was only about three miles from the college where a new road of two double lanes in each direction, separated by a wide grass barrier and a traffic circle of grass at the lowest point on the road, had been put down only a few years before. It was very modern. The road down to the traffic circle was a long half mile downward slope with another half mile slope upwards on the other side of the circle. I'd developed a way of cycling fast on the downward slope, reaching over thirty miles an hour as I took a long sweep around the circle, using my momentum to cycle hard up the other slope so I could reach the top out of breath but triumphant as I finished the ride to College. I'd done it many times on other similar banks, passing double-decker buses lumbering up Billingham Bank road, passing in the outside lane as was proper for passing traffic. I didn't think anything of it so when I saw a car slowly struggling and backfiring on the upper slope I overtook and sped past it. I don't remember the accident but it was seen by my friend Terry Cox

87

Survivor

cycling down the upper slope behind me. He told me that the car picked up speed and swung out and hit me and I went across the body of the car on to the roadway. The car stopped and people looked out at me and accelerated away.

Terry said he didn't recognize me because of all the blood but he recognized my wrecked bike and knew it was me. A workmens van had been just behind me and they stopped and picked me up and put me on the floor of the van, benches along the side with working men on the way home from work, and turned around and went at high speed to Middlesbrough General Hospital some ten miles away. I do remember some of that, my eyes bleary and my face and body in pain, hearing a mixture of the men cursing the driver that had hit me mixed with compassionate reassurances that I would be all right, that I'd be at the hospital soon.

Middlesbrough General hospital had been the major hospital for the people of Tees-side injured in the bombing raids during the second World War and it must have been that some of the surgeons and nurses around me had experiences from the time that saved me and had me wondering why they were being so kind to me as I was held down on the operating table under bright lights, holding my hands, stitching me, telling me to grip my hands if the pain of the injections of local pain killers and stitching was too much, that they would stop for me to scream, encouraged me to scream, before they would continue. They talked to me; telling me I was a brave lad, keep screaming they said, we'll be finished soon. They found a deep cut down the center of my tongue and were going to stitch that but I clamped my mouth shut at that prospect and screamed and screamed. The surgeon gripped my shoulder and told me to relax, he wouldn't do it. He said it would heal on its own. At some point I must have passed out taking that curious scar in my tongue into the future because I didn't become aware until three days later in a hospital bed with bandages and dressings covering my face and blocking my nose. I'd had dozens of stitches and my nose reconstructed and I'd been awake and talking for those three days but I had no memory of it and to this day it is a blank in my mind. I was told later it was shock.

Survivor

When I became aware it was afternoon, sunlight coming in the windows, my mother beside the bed holding my hand and stroking it, crying and saying to me I was going to be alright. At that I felt I was dying and I should just let it happen. That feeling didn't last long because I saw Father Green, the rustle of his cassock comforting me, striding down the ward toward me. He reached me and stood looking down at me and said with a smile: "John, you look a bloody mess," and at that I relaxed and knew I was going to live.

I was released from the hospital three days later after the cotton stuffing in my nose had been taken out, disgusting odor, letting me breathe properly. I didn't become thoroughly demoralized until I was back in Derby Street looking in a mirror. My good looks were gone, my blue eyes looking at stitched scars. I looked like a monster. I was plunged into despair wondering how I could live with such a fate, deciding I wanted to go back to work, to be among people who would be kind to me.

Chapter 6

As I got on the bus the following Monday morning it was overcast and there was a chill in the air with a light rain falling on me. I was going through instances of despair with an internal determination not to let this grind me down, thinking to myself other people had it worse and I shouldn't feel sorry for myself. I'd cleaned myself as best I could, shaving some of my skin with difficulty, not that there was much hair there anyway, in anguish over the swollen areas around the stitches, the cystic acne combining with the wounds causing me grief. The stitches they had told me would dissolve in time. I would still be scarred. I would still have acne even worse than before, infections to tackle.

The men at the bus stop didn't stare at me. Some looked at me with a kind compassion in their eyes. A few looked at me with pity and those were the ones that raised a fury in me. I knew I was still the same person. The accident hadn't taken away my mind and thoughts.

On the way to work I managed to get a front seat on the upper deck of the bus and I looked ahead onto Norton Road thinking of my wrecked bike and what I'd need to do to get it back into shape. I could get the parts from Curry's bike shop. I had the money. I'd missed the last week of night school but that wasn't any trouble at all. I didn't have any important exams to do and I could catch up. I'd just have to travel by bus for a while.

When I arrived at the Standardisation Laboratory I was uncomfortable by all the attention I was getting, wanting just to be accepted, hoping that by not looking at myself in a mirror I could forget it and focus on titrations. The morning went by without me getting any work done, Mr. Redman and Dave Nicholson telling me to sit in a chair in Mr. Redman's office because Mr. Rudd and Roger and Clive were coming to see me and others in 'O' Building wanted to give me their support and best wishes for recovery. At first I thought I was going to lose my job but that soon faded. I belonged. They all made that clear. The gloom began to lift from me and I was even able to laugh and tell of the workmen in the van and Middlesbrough General Hospital. Mr. Redman ordered

Survivor

sandwiches and tea from the cafeteria as the others went to lunch. The unusual nature of that surprised me. I'd been dreading going to the cafeteria and somehow he had known that. While we were eating at his desk his kindness and softly aggressive voice made me feel safe. He told me that I.C.I. was going to give me two weeks off work on full pay so that I could recover. It would start at the end of the sick week I was still on. That frightened me at first until his words began to penetrate, that I was a valuable employee and they wanted me to have time to get over the shock, that I'd be on sick leave and my National Insurance stamps would be paid for me, which would mean that I'd have even a bit more salary deposited in the bank, that I shouldn't worry myself, they'd all look forward to me coming back. He explained that the Standardisation Laboratory was being moved to a larger more modern laboratory on the third floor of 'N' building, nearer to the cafeteria, and that I wasn't expected to help in the move, with all that dust and clutter, and he smiled at me, compassion evident in his kindly eyes, as he told me to go home and do what I needed to do and my job would be waiting for me in 'N' building when I came back. Dave Nicholson and the colliery lad would do extra time if it was needed. My eyes looked fine. The titrations would be there for me in a couple of weeks.

I had to walk down to the main road to get a Corporation bus back to Stockton, eager to go work on my bike. My father had gone to work. Patricia was at work and Mary and Tommy and Terry were in school. My mother and I had some rare time alone together as she sat on my bed watching me taking apart the wreck of my bike and writing down the parts I'd need. She was amazed that I'd been given over two weeks off on full pay. I loved my mother even more than ever then, having the feeling that she could look past my injuries and see me as I really was. She kept on bringing me cups of tea as I worked and we talked about what I was going to do with the two weeks. I hadn't really formulated anything up to that point until she started talking to me about going to church to pray and I looked up and saw tears in her eyes. I wanted so much to tell her I was going to be alright and that began the growth of an ambition to

Survivor

cycle to Grandma in Roscommon and pray in the Sacred Heart church there.

She seemed relieved at that; as though we both shared the same thought, that I'd be better off out of the way of my father. I assured her that I'd get the money from the bank for the two weeks rent and food while I was gone and she cried some more and then laughed and told me that she'd been to the rental TV store at the end of the High Street and when I got back we'd have our own television. It would be a good size and put on the shelf above where Spot used to sleep. We talked of Spot for a while and how she was a good dog and had followed me everywhere when I was young and how I had cried for days when she was hit by a car and died.

That being 1961 the television would be black and white and could only get the BBC and the Tyne-Tees independent channel that would have commercials. Most people rented a television in those days. Only the rich people could actually buy one. But it was a step up and it would be in the house when I got back and she said it was all due to me.

The next couple of days went by in a flurry of repair and preparation. Mr. Redman had told me my two weeks off would start after the current week which meant I had almost three weeks to plan for. I was back at Curry's bicycle shop several times and I was taken aback that they knew about my accident, even more so the people I didn't even know stopping me walking on the High Street, looking at my face and telling me I was a brave lad. I wasn't quite sure what bravery had to do with it but I liked that they cared to talk to me and cheer me up. I went to the Army and Navy store and bought a small tent and a primus stove and a set of camping pots and pans. I bought a new very large saddle bag to attach to the back of the seat of my bike and straps to secure the tent on top of that. I had a long journey ahead of me. I was going to do some camping.

I'd decided I was not only going to go to Roscommon. I planned to cycle another forty miles north of Ballybohan to the holy shrine at Knock and pray for the Virgin Mary to intercede with God and grant me a miracle. I didn't share those thoughts with anyone, not even Patricia or my Aunt Josie. They were private thoughts, just between me and God, thoughts and prayers that would take me

92

Survivor

though until I got to the holy shrine. I had maps and the times of the ferry departures from Liverpool to Dublin, twelve hours on a ship across the Irish Sea. The longest ride would be from Stockton across the Pennines and then down to Liverpool.

The Pennines are a long mountain chain dividing the North East coast of England from the North West coast. On my maps I saw that no point on the road would be higher elevation than where I'd been on the Lyke Wake walk. There would be places on the hills where I would have to get off my bike and push to the top of the hill. Once I reached the highest points at about the ninety mile point it would be much easier going down toward Liverpool. As it turned out I managed to reach that highest point on the first day and camped that night by the side of the road. As I cooked myself eggs and pork sausage with my new primus stove and set of pans I continued to pray for a miracle at Knock. At times I'd cried as I cycled, not feeling sorry for myself, more in relief that I had a firm objective ahead of me and all I had to do was keep cycling.

The landscape was beautiful with heather blooming on the hills and pastures with sheep grazing in the valleys, small villages miles apart, streams running under small bridges, an occasional car passing me, sometimes a horn beeping me and waving at me as they passed, encouraging me, friendship from strangers, and that warmed my heart. I had another fifty five miles to go the next day so I was able to take plenty of time looking around me as I descended from the hills and through the industrial towns of Manchester and surrounding cities, heart of the Industrial Revolution, gladdening me as I was awed by the mile upon mile of foundries and factories and roads and railway lines, houses that seemed to go on forever.

By the time I reached the ferry terminal in Liverpool I still had several hours to wait to buy a ticket so I sat by the dock smelling the sea air, watching and listening to the seagulls calling and swirling around the docks. The ferry ship was much larger than I had expected, with several decks, and pubs on board and restaurants and crowds of people having a good time. They were mainly Irish people going home for a holiday with many children and old people. The ship sailed at ten in the evening and an

93

Survivor

announcement let us know the Irish Sea was calm that night and the crossing would take about ten hours. We would make good time. I'd suppose calm was a relative term because within hours the swaying of the decks had men coming out of the pub area on the lower deck, resting on the rail and being sick into the ocean. It didn't bother me at all. I enjoyed seeing the children who were running all over the ship screaming and yelling and having a generally good time. Sometime during the night singing began in the pubs and spread out onto the decks, Irish songs, singing of going home. I wanted to join in and my heart ached that I'd never been taught to sing. I didn't sleep at all that night or wanted to, joining other people at the rail on the upper deck in the early morning looking for the first signs of Dublin coming into view. The pubs were closed and the singing had died down and the younger children were cuddled up sleeping in blankets with their parents on chairs and benches and just about any open space.

The ship docked in the center of Dublin and I didn't waste any time getting out of the city and on the road. I had another ninety one miles to get to Roscommon and Ballybohan but it would be all mainly easy going and I didn't expect I'd have to get off my bike to push. It was an overcast day but my spirit soared as I breathed in the fresh Irish air, passing by pastures with cows grazing in the fields, sometimes getting a whiff of cow shit in the fields and grinning to myself, remembering my childhood in Ballybohan and taking the cows down the road to the Dolan milking sheds. I prayed constantly in my mind, pleading with God to grant me a miracle, to heal my face. My tears had dried away on reaching Ireland. As I crossed the Shannon river at Athlone, into the province of Connaught, twenty more miles to go, I felt I was truly home, I was where I belonged, where I had my grandmother and ancestors who would look over me.

In that strange way of Roscommon in those days, before the ordinary people had telephones, word had gone on ahead of me, I'd been seen on the road north from Athlone, cars and bicycles and people walking had let my grandmother know I was on my way. She already had potatoes in the pot hanging above the turf fire, cabbage already cooked kept warm in a pot beside the embers,

94

Survivor

buttermilk in a large jug on the table, bacon rashers in a pan ready to be cooked as soon as I walked in. She made a great fuss of me, marveling at how I'd bicycled that whole way by myself, not even commenting about my face, just saying she had lit a candle in the church to thank the saints that I had not been killed. My bed in my old room was already made up for me and when I told her I wanted to go to Knock after praying in the Sacred Heart church the next morning she was delighted. She thought I was going to pray in thanks for my survival. I didn't tell her about my prayers for a miracle. That was too deep inside me to share with anyone. I slept for a long time that night, so long that it wasn't until afternoon that my grandmother got on her old fashioned bike and we rode into Roscommon town so I could say prayers in the Sacred Heart church. I put off going to Knock until the next day because there were people coming over that evening to welcome me home.

Knock is forty one miles northeast of Roscommon in the County of Mayo. It was there in 1879 that an apparition of the Virgin Mary, St. Joseph, and St. John the Evangelist appeared for several hours one evening to fifteen people, men, women and children. Investigations and church inquiries led to the place being a site of pilgrimage. Miracles and favors from God had been reported there since, with cripples leaving their crutches at the shrine.

When I arrived I was scandalized at the stalls selling all sorts of trinkets so I parked my bike by the wall of the church and walked onto the area where there was a moving procession of people saying the rosary in a route around the shrine, a stage on which a mass would be said still empty. I took my rosary beads out of my pocket and joined the procession, looking down at the ground as I walked, praying aloud with the decades of the rosary, in my mind pleading with all my heart for God to grant me a miracle, to heal my face. After several rounds of the shrine I began to look up and it was then that I saw the crippled children in wheelchairs in rows just in front of the stage; so many crippled children. I underwent a revelation. From one instant to the next I changed the pleading in my mind. I began to pray to God that he heal just one of those crippled children, not me, and I would accept my face would

95

not be healed. In the innocence of my age I accepted in my heart that I'd have to live with the scars until I was at least thirty, not imagining that I'd ever live older than that. A wondrous thing happened. By the end of the Mass it was as if a burden had been lifted from my shoulders and the grief that had tormented me was gone. I was able to lift my head and look forward, in the hope that my prayers had been heard and a crippled child would walk. That experience has been with me all my life.

As I left Knock I wanted to keep that special wonderful feeling with me for a while so I cycled west toward the north Mayo coast road, past the town of Ballina and on to Bangor Erris. It's a relatively uninhabited part of Ireland, with only small farms and hamlets here and there, beautiful with land and history evoking poetry in my thoughts, thinking of my grandfather and all of my cousins who had never been born, of heroism and times past. I camped on green grass by the side of the river in Bangor Erris, asking first if I could in the single pub there, rejoicing in hearing the Irish language spoken there, taking it as a good sign seeing a heron standing on one leg by the water barely fifty feet from me. A very young girl came out from the pub to give me fresh brown eggs and a canteen of milk. She talked to me in Irish but I was only able to respond to her to say thank you and it's a beautiful evening before she giggled and ran back to the pub. There were only a few dozen houses in Bangor Erris so I must have been talked about that night. The next morning the girl's mother brought me more eggs and milk and talked to me in English. When she found out my name was Fahey she became very friendly and talked with me for a while, drinking the tea I made, asking about my family, telling me there was a Fahy village, smaller than Bangor Erris further down the coast road as I headed south toward Mulrany and Westport.

It was during that talk, feeling close to the history of Ireland, that a thought waiting to be born came to my mind, and as I cycled south on the coast road it came to a firm decision. I'd known for some time that because my father and grandparents had been born in Ireland I was entitled to apply for Irish citizenship. I resolved to do it.

Survivor

For the next couple of days, as I cycled back to Ballybohan, that occupied my thoughts.

My grandmother helped me. She went with me into town and took me to the records office where she talked for ages to the woman there about people they knew until to my amazement an assistant came up to the counter with a freshly written copy of my father's birth certificate. I was given the information about writing to get an application form from an office in Dublin and was thrilled at how easy it was going to be. My grandmother insisted that we go to the Central, a pub on the Square, center of Roscommon town, where I had a cup of tea and she had a 'hot whiskey'. She had had tremors of her hands and head since her early forties and her doctor had told her she had a mild form of Parkinson's disease and the whisky would help. It was a mix of whisky and sugar and hot water and indeed after she drank one of them her tremors died down.

We left the Central amid a shaking of hands as the room became more crowded with men coming in from the cattle market.

My journey back to England was an entirely different sort of experience for me. My mood was much lighter, more confident, looking forward and planning as if I'd never had an accident. I was fascinated coming into Liverpool when the ship came in to a separate dock first to unload hundreds of young cattle from below the decks, then a little later at the dock where we would get off the ship seeing nuns at the quayside looking for pregnant girls getting off the ship. Ireland still had those laws about unmarried mothers and many fled to England where they would not be separated from their baby and put into an institution.

By the time I got to Derby Street I still had almost a week left so I spent that time reading and thinking and going to see my Aunt Josie. By the time I got to my job in 'N' Building I was fully ready for titrations. It was a much bigger laboratory on the third floor with huge windows looking out for miles at the surrounding area. I was late for registration for classes but they let me do it anyway. I could catch up. My classmates were just as before, laughter and joking, not mentioning the state of my face, just insisting that I join them in darts sessions. In some ways I felt as if it were camaraderie for a soldier coming back from war.

Survivor

So as it came to a close for that year my life had settled into a routine. And if at times my drunken father would come into my room late at night, going into my pockets and cursing at only finding coins, hitting at me until I'd scream, too weak to fight back, I'd go to sleep trying to dream of escaping, knowing I had my Irish passport hidden with my Irish grammar books and my bank book beneath me as I slept.

The voyage to Knock had given me the fortitude and stimulus to keep looking forward, seeking a silver lining in the darkest cloud, hope sustaining me as I tackled each problem I faced. What I had read in the Kraft-Ebbing book still troubled me but I tried to ignore those dire predictions by relegating them to a far distant future, a problem to be tackled when the time came. I had more immediate concerns. Patricia had pointed out to me one day that when I walked only my right arm swung with my left arm hanging. I didn't feel anything wrong with my left arm so I began to focus on swinging it in synchrony and that seemed to work after a while. I decided I wouldn't worry about it; I'd just focus my attention on it.

I'd begun weekly visits to a Doctors office, called a surgery, on Norton Road. There were three doctors there and all I had to do is turn up and wait with other people for my name to be called. The two doctors who were treating me were Dr. Webster and Dr. Scarff. In the months leading up to my one year point with I.C.I. the stitches had mainly dissolved but had left scarring and bloody pustules, lumps of tissue along my jaw, distress when I looked in a mirror. I was told to cut out all sugar foods and stop using salt because of high blood pressure. I adjusted quickly to that, giving up my favorite apple pie and hot custard, only putting vinegar on my fish and chips. I was put on to a regimen of oral and topical greasy antibiotics. Finally I was set up with weekly UV radiation treatments to burn off the upper layers of my skin.

Throughout it all my classmates and the people I worked with never commented on it with me, not treating me any different than they had before the accident. That made it much easier for me. I was able to focus on titrations and schoolwork and reading to fully occupy my time. By January Dr. Scarff told me that I would have to get used to never having a normal face and that broke my heart for

98

a long time afterward. That turned me even more to learning as much chemistry as I could, always seeking answers, continuing to believe in better years ahead.

Though it was difficult catching up on my studies I set myself the objective of taking G.C.E. 'A' levels in June 1962. That would be the time when I would have been normally taking them if I had been allowed to stay at St. Mary's College full time. The minimum requirements to apply for university were five 'O' levels and two 'A' levels. I already had plenty of 'O' levels so I planned to take 'A' levels in Chemistry, Physics and Mathematics.

Marjorie Naisbitt and I started going to the cinema together once a week. I liked her so much and she liked me, her infectious laughter always being able to put me in a good mood. It seemed to me then I was living a normal life. She sustained me, helped me accommodate to myself, talked with me of many things. She had the ambition to get her library qualifications and then travel abroad. She talked about 'au pair' Nanny Jobs and we'd joke about the best and worst that could come to and she'd show me the advertisements in magazines she was reading. It would be the highlight of my week to go see a film with her at a cinema. I always let her choose the film and we'd share what it would cost, going for fish and chips afterward.

I reached the age of eighteen March 4, 1962. It passed by with little fanfare. Patricia and Marjorie each bought me a birthday card. I treasured those cards for years.

Whenever I would go to Stockton Public Library on Wellington Street I'd first go to a central section in the main room where recently returned novels were stacked along a sloping shelf. At the end of March I came across a novel that had a profound impact on my life. The title attracted me and after perusing a few pages I was immediately drawn to it. The book was by a writer called Mary Renault and was titled 'Fire from Heaven'. It was a historical novel about the early life of Alexander the Great. That led to me another of her novels: 'The Persian Boy', about Alexander's later life and military campaigns. As I read and reread those novels my heart soared. As I read about the young Alexander and his companions, other young men of the Macedonian aristocracy, being

Survivor

taught by Aristotle, and his beloved friend Hephaestion, going out to conquer the known world, heroism and honor and dignity, bringing respect and architecture and great public works to the regions they conquered, sending wagon trains of observations and documents and samples back to Aristotle, their love for each other making observers compare them to Achilles and Patroclus, eased the aching in my heart, let me know what I had been looking for.

Of course I then went looking for books on Achilles and Patroclus, my senses and thoughts as if they were singing to me as I read, telling me this is right, this is how you feel, Kraft-Ebbing is full of rubbish. I felt I'd had the equivalent of Aristotle with the priests at St. Mary's College, learning of honor and ethics and respect for learning, though as my first excitement at reading about those ancient times faded I brought myself back down to earth. It was over two and a half thousand years in the past and even by the remotest chance I could find my own Hephaestion we would be caught and put into jail. The sort of love I thought of had become illegal.

I was travelling mainly by bus to work and night school by that time. There was always a lot of traffic on the roads and the thought of another accident plagued me. I'd ride my bike for pleasure on weekends when there would be less traffic and I could choose quieter roads, sometimes going out into the countryside north of Stockton and around Yarm. My life had again become routine. As I'd grown taller and kept giving my mother money Saturday morning my father's attacks on me became less frequent though he still often cursed at me and derided me and said I wasn't his son.

I'd even been able to go back to studying in my parlor room, no longer frightened he'd invade and punch me. Even when it did happen I just let it. Better me than my mother or sisters or brothers. For some reason he'd also stopped burning my books as long as I kept them in my room. He'd been getting regular work on the Barber-Greene. He was still drunk all the time. It seemed as if the rental television had calmed him down. Though he still went into rages and broke furniture at times he never attacked the television. He just hit my mother and me.

100

Survivor

Patricia had Billy, who would come into the house to pick her up and look menacingly at my father. Billy was big and muscular and in the building trades. My father wouldn't hit Patricia when Billy was there.

The Summer 1962 London University G.C.E. examinations were held at Stockton-Billingham Technical College in June. Mr. Redman had sent me to the company library after I arrived at work for each day before I took an examination, that being another company policy. The weather was pleasant and windows had been opened to let in the breezes. I did pass in my three subjects but only at the 'A' level in chemistry, being given an 'O' level pass in physics and mathematics. That hurt but I rationalized to myself what with a job and night school and my accident it was only a setback and I could take them again at the next opportunity in January 1963. So I relaxed from my studies, wanting to spend all my time in the Standardisation Laboratory, reading more science fiction, cycling in the countryside on weekends, thinking about what I'd learned from books.

I liked my work, always arriving early, never missed a day. I knew my job was important, Winchesters of standard solutions that I had helped standardize going out each morning, delicious lunches in the cafeteria and often dinner in the cafeteria on those days I rode my bike in, so that I wouldn't have to go back to Derby Street, could cycle out into the countryside. On days it would rain I'd get the bus and go to the Wellington Street Library after my cafeteria dinner, giving myself time enough until my father would have gone out to the pubs. I discovered a small room, next to the room with old men reading newspapers and smoking cigarettes, where an old lady at a desk could give my access to past G.C.E. examinations. I couldn't take them out but was able to study them at a table in that room. I was usually the only one there and it was very quiet and I'd often enough become engrossed in those papers until closing time, scribbling on notepads, the time seeming to fly by.

I registered for the autumn schedule of classes at Stockton-Billingham Technical College in September and went back to my regular day release day and two evenings. I was determined to get my three 'A' levels by January.

101

Survivor

The rumblings of atomic war had been filling the newspapers and news channels on television throughout August and September. Russia and America were threatening each other. By the second week of October it had grown to confrontation. It was the Cuban Missile Crisis. Day by day as Russian ships headed to Cuba, war seemed to be about almost inevitable. The talk in I.C.I. was somber. We all knew that I.C.I. would be the first to be hit by an atomic bomb, being about the center of the nearest industrial region to the Russian border. For over a week our work slowed to a low pace. The wide windows of our third floor laboratory had a clear view out toward the Tees estuary and the North Sea. We had a view of distant bombers, two at a time, every twenty minutes, heading out over the sea and vanishing from view into the cloud cover. We always had at least one person standing watching at the windows, timing when returning bombers would break cloud cover coming back. We knew that if the bombers did not come back we'd have minutes left until an atomic bomb would hit us. Everyone was remarkably calm; talking that it was better that it would be quick, not horrible like people slowly dying of radiation in country areas. It went on for thirteen days until by October 28 America and Russia had reached agreement on de-escalating the threats. It did convince me that even the threat of atomic war is madness and only madmen would contemplate it. I've never had reason to change that point of view.

In January 1963 I took the 'A' G.C.E. examinations and passed at 'A' level in all three. University of London passes in chemistry, physics, pure and applied mathematics. I was happy with that, even talking about my success back in Derby Street. That was daring of me but I wanted to see my father's reaction. He disparaged me, telling me it was all book learning, but I took that as a victory. He didn't attack me as he would have done in previous years.

I went to see my Aunt Josie to show her the certificate and to tell her that I now had the qualifications to apply to university. She had raisin scones cooking in the oven, butter on the table, when she asked if I'd told my dad. At my answer she sat down with a worried look on her face. "John", she said, "don't tell him any more…trust me...we'll change your address to here in Patterdale Avenue. Don't let him know what you are doing". Then she laughed and said: "it won't look unusual to the postman...we're all Faheys here anyhow". She drummed it into me. That I should keep my mouth shut. Don't talk to him about going to university. I'll talk to your mother. And so it was the following Saturday morning Josie met with me at the Empire cinema to pick my mother up after her work to go across the High Street to the main post office where they filled out the paper that changed my address to Patterdale Avenue. Josie liked my mother and my mother liked and trusted Josie. They went shopping and talking into the market, telling me to go off and have a good day with my friends, just keep my mouth shut around my father.

Nobody we knew had ever taken 'A' levels or applied to university so my Aunt Josie's clear thinking had saved me from an unknown disaster. I did need advice on what to do next so I turned to Mr. Redman for that. Within days I had the university application form, the UCCA, Universities Central Council on Admissions, and went to Patterdale Avenue because I wanted Josie with me as I filled it out. I was allowed to apply to four universities. I applied to the Universities of Manchester, Leeds and Sheffield then on a bold whim I put down the University of St. Andrews in Scotland. I didn't think I had a chance of getting in there but I put it down anyway. My friend Steve from night school had gone there in September and had laughed with joy in telling me he had got in. "It's the best," he said, "if you can't get into Oxford or Cambridge then get into St. Andrews. It's the Scottish Oxford". I'd learned it was an ancient university and very prestigious. Steve was from an upper class family. I was not. But I put it down anyway. That meant I had also to send evidence of my 'O' level and 'A' level passes to the Scottish Universities Entrance Board so I did that along with my UCCA application to the four universities.

Mr. Redman had told me that if a university was going to consider me for a place I'd get a letter setting me up for a personal interview and so I should get my mind ready for some one day train trips. I'd get the day off for such interview days. I'd get full salary as always. He wished me good luck.

Survivor

My nineteenth birthday went by without notice and March went on into April as the days became warmer and my hopes and dreams were tied to getting at least one interview.

Months had gone by without a letter inviting me for an interview and my initial excitement began to die down. Mr. Redman encouraged me to think positive, telling me they were waiting for the June applicants, it being unusual for someone to apply early in the year. Then almost suddenly, to me at least, from April to May, I got three invitations from Manchester, Leeds and Sheffield.

My excitement had my heart pounding as I scrubbed and cleaned myself in the Turkish Baths the evening before my train trip to Leeds. I'd made sure my white shirt and trousers were neatly ironed, a new tie setting it off nicely. My shoes were gleaming with black polish. I didn't have a coat and I didn't think a sweater would be appropriate but it was going to be a mild day and I wouldn't need a coat. Mr. Redman had given me a pound note for if I needed a taxi, gruffly, waving off my thanks. My face I couldn't do much about. Dr. Scarff had discontinued the antibiotics and UV radiation treatment at the beginning of the year, telling me to give it time to heal, eat a lot of vegetables and fruit, and get out into the open air.

I enjoyed the train ride from Stockton to Leeds, changing in York, looking out the window, feeling my life changing yet again. Though I was trembling during the interview it went well and was over within an hour. A week later a letter arrived at Patterdale Avenue for me with an offer to enter the B.Sc. Chemistry program, a three year program. I was thrilled, taking it to work to show Mr. Redman. I was going to write back to accept and he told me not to. "You've got another three out there", he said, "give them all a chance at you", and he laughed a good hearty laugh with pleasure in my happiness.

By the beginning of August I'd had my interviews at Sheffield and Manchester and been offered places in their three year B.Sc. programs. I was on the point of accepting the offer from the University of Manchester when a stunning letter came to me from the University of St. Andrews. It was stunning to me because it wasn't to invite me for an interview. It was a direct acceptance of

104

Survivor

me into the B.Sc. Chemistry program, four years that would lead to an Honours B.Sc., a higher level of degree. Mr. Redman and the other people in 'N' Building and 'O' Building were all excited for me, urging me to write back and accept. So I did that.

The University of St. Andrews is an ancient university, the third oldest university in the English speaking world, founded between 1410 and 1413, just after Oxford and Cambridge. The original campus is in the town of St. Andrews, in the county of Fife, on the coast. The larger campus, at which I had been accepted, was further north, in Dundee, by the river Tay. The letter advised me that my tuition fees would be paid for by the university and that I would need to apply to my local council for a grant to pay my living expenses. As I showed the letter to Josie she picked up an envelope from the sideboard beside her and handed it to me. "I already got it for you," she said, "from my friend when you were accepted at Leeds." She smiled at me. "I've already filled most of it out weeks ago.....now all we have to do is put in St. Andrews and a few other things and we can mail it." As I sat at the kitchen table writing in the last details I saw my mother's signature and my father's signature at the end of the document. I looked up in surprise and she grinned at me: "...that's your mother's signature alright...I took it down to the Empire for her to sign it...and I signed it for your dad, after all I am his sister and a Fahey and I signed his name because he's non compos mentis", laughing, "he's been non compos mentis for a long time." Josie always had the ability to surprise me. I never knew she knew some Latin. She went on to tell me the application for the grant would have to be done twice a year but not to worry, she and my mother would take care of it. Just don't tell my father. She took the form from me, sealed it into the envelope, told me she'd mail it the next morning, and smiled a mischievous knowing smile at me, ruffling my hair, '..go on then now," she said, "..go become famous..I'm proud of you".

Less than two weeks later a letter came telling me I had been granted a Bursary by Durham County Council. It would be waiting for me at the Bursars office at the beginning of each term. It was almost exactly the same amount of money for three ten week terms that I was getting at I.C.I. but nothing during the summers. That was no problem for me. I was an ici person. I could leave university on a Friday and be back in the laboratory on a Monday. I was thrilled and excited and overwhelmed. I'd done it. I was going to Scotland. I was escaping.

Soon after I received confirmation of my acceptance by the university, and where I had to go to get my bursary. The package included information about the university and the chemistry department and the start of term. As a first year student I was be termed a bejant; a name from the middle ages. I had to send them a request for accommodation which could be a residence hall or lodging in a home in the town. I chose lodging, being uncertain about the prospect of a residence hall, thinking it would be for an upper class of person and lodging would be more for someone like me from the working class. I sat with Josie going through the information I'd been sent and she pointed out students wearing a red gown with a velvet collar and we laughed together as I pointed out it would only be for ceremonial occasions and debates and surely I wouldn't be expected to wear it going to class. I was to be automatically a member of the Student Union and there were many different clubs and societies I could join, a pub in the Student Union building and that amazed me, sports facilities, events and dances which were called 'hops'. I couldn't imagine that at all. Billy would take Patricia to dances but I'd never been to a dance. Josie assured me I'd love it, probably not ballroom dancing but more likely dancing to rock and roll music, that being what young people were into nowadays. She was so happy that I was going to Scotland, a Celtic country like Ireland, but with mountains much larger. I'd been sent a map and we saw that Dundee was on the east coast facing the North Sea just like Tees-side and the river flowing out to the sea was called the Firth of Tay. It looked much wider than the Tees. Thirty eight miles south of Dundee was the Scottish city of Edinburgh, located on the Firth of Forth, another very wide river. We found out that Gaelic was still spoken in some parts of the Highlands and it was very like Irish. It suddenly occurred to us almost at the same time that surely there wouldn't be very many English people there and we had a merry time laughing about that.

Survivor

When I received the letter telling me where my lodging was, the weekly money to be paid directly to the lady of the house, it all began to seem so definite and real to me. The lady only put up one student at a time so I'd be the only one. The address was near a high point in Dundee, close to a place called The Law. In a geology book in Wellington Street library I read that the Law was over five hundred above sea level and was the tip of an extinct volcano.

I still had several weeks to prepare so I decided to finally buy a suit from Alexander's. I'd been budgeting carefully and I had plenty of money so one day I boldly walked in, past the displays in guineas, and walked up to a man with a cloth measuring tape around his neck. He was a very nice man as I explained I needed a suit to go to university with. He measured me, a very strange experience, talking about the kind of suit I should have, and talked of fabrics and styles. I'd seen one in the window I liked and he showed me a rack of them. I picked one that cost ten guineas, which was ten pounds and ten shillings, and wrote him a cheque from my bank account. I rarely had occasion to do that but since I was in a posh store that seemed to be the posh thing to do. After being fitted with the suit and looking at myself in a tall mirror he explained he was measuring me again so that more work had to be done on it so it would fit me perfectly and that pleased me immensely, that he was taking so much time with me. He told me to come back in three days and it would be ready.

Patricia borrowed a camera and took a photo of me in the suit standing in Derby Street. I've had that photo with me since. In my mind I see not only myself but my sister Patricia smiling at me as she took my picture. It was a happy time for both of us.

My final days in I.C.I. seemed to be filled with people coming by the Standardisation Laboratory to congratulate me, even Mr. Redman's superiors. I didn't think they'd ever noticed me. The personnel man filled out leave of absence papers with me and gave me an account of the accumulated I.C.I. voting shares I had. I'd quite forgotten about that, not really looking at the shares each year, knowing it was to be held in trust for me until I was twenty one. But seeing the amount on paper and being told I was still an I.C.I. employee even while I was away at university and that my National

Survivor

Insurance Stamps would be paid for while I was away, filled me with a deep sense of belonging.

In the days before I was to leave I bought a large cheap grey suitcase from Stockton market to pack my suit and clothes and favorite books and towels and shaving kit. I put my papers and bank book and my certificates and letters and photographs and passport into large brown envelopes and put those on top of my clothes. My mother and Patricia had tried to persuade me to not tell my father. They told me to just leave one day and not come back. But I knew deep in my heart that he really was my father and I wanted to give him one last chance to be proud of me. That was a mistake. He seemed to be in a good mood when he came back from the pub that night. I tried to tell him I'd been accepted into University. He exploded into a rage, punching me in the face, kicking me, roaring at me, cursing me that I was a bastard, he was going to kick all that nonsense out of me, he was taking me out of I.C.I., they'd put all that high faluting nonsense into me...he'd have me digging ditches before the week was out...he wouldn't let me go...I needed his permission...I was too young to sign anything. He left me sprawled on the floor, my mother crying, screaming throughout the house from my sisters and brothers. When I looked at myself the next morning my right eye was heavily bruised, my lip was split with dried blood below it onto my chin. I had lost a tooth on the right side of my lower jaw. He'd given me his answer. He wasn't proud of me.

As I was trying to clean my face at the kitchen sink late the following morning Patricia walked into the kitchen and gently took the washcloth and began to clean the dried blood from my face. She'd taken the afternoon off work, Dad was going to be coming home early, Mam was going to the pub to delay him, there wasn't much time, and I should go right now. So I left Derby Street, a suitcase hanging from my left hand, pushing the handlebars of my bike with the other hand, Patricia going on ahead to look up and down the alleyway to make sure our father was not within sight, waving me forward. I walked to Stockton Railway Station, bought a ticket and soon was on a train to Scotland, escaping to freedom and another life.

108

On the way to Edinburgh, where I would change trains for Dundee, I had great anticipations but at times I would feel sad, thinking that I had abandoned my mother and sisters and brothers. Many years later Patricia was to tell me that the longer I stayed away gave her and Mary hope that one day they could escape too.

Chapter 7

I began to relax as I sat in my train seat looking out the window at the countryside. Newcastle-on-Tyne was the first major city we stopped at, with a large busy station, people getting on and off, doors slamming with shouts of all aboard, eagerness in me that soon we would be crossing the border into Scotland. I'd finished reading the newspapers I'd bought in Stockton station. My mind kept casting back to Derby Street and what was happening there. When Patricia and I were young, being close in age and together, people used to call us 'irish twins' and indeed as the train travelled further north I felt an invisible link between us, undiminished by distance, causing my heart to ache in fear for her.

When the train reached Edinburgh, exciting me as we crossed the Firth of Forth, seeing a city of grey stone ahead, I had to take down my suitcase from the overhead rack and get my bike from the luggage car and take them along several platforms to reach the coast train for Dundee. I had over an hour for the connection so I had time to buy a cup of tea and a ham and egg sandwich, enchanted by the Scots burr and the smile of the girl handing it over to me. I tried to start a conversation but she had other customers so I contented myself by sitting on a nearby bench and listening to the talk of people at the counter and passing by, pleasing me, making me feel I was truly in another country.

The train to Dundee, taking me almost another forty miles north, was slow, stopping at towns along the coast, so it was late afternoon when I saw the Tay rail bridge, over two and a half miles long, curving out over the Tay and straight into Dundee on the other side of the river. I had the impression of distant grey buildings rising to a peak. I'd not had much time to read about Dundee but I'd read it was famous for 'jute, jam, and journalism', had a history of shipbuilding, and a long history of wars and conflicts with England.

The taxi driver was friendly and helpful, getting my bike into the back of the taxi while I sat beside him in the front, talking to me about Dundee as he drove me to my destination. He was almost incomprehensible so I just nodded and agreed with him, suspecting

Survivor

from his frequent chuckles that he was entertaining me with exaggeration of his Dundee Scots accent. As the taxi climbed the streets toward the Law I soon realized my bike was not going to be used much. The streets were too steep. My landlady was a very small frail old woman, smaller even than my sister Mary. She showed me my bedroom on the ground floor and told me in the evenings I could watch television with her in the living room. It was four pounds a week and included breakfast. I assured her I didn't want to be a burden on her and all I needed for breakfast was tea and buttered toast, being that I had to avoid sugar and salt. She seemed troubled by that, talking of lads needing a good breakfast, so I told her I'd be getting good meals at the university. I was confident the university cafeteria, like at I.C.I., would have a full breakfast service with a range of choices. She was much more comprehensible than the taxi driver. It was a nice bedroom. It was a safe room. My father would not burst in to hit me there. I felt that was all behind me, not being aware of the power of frightening memories.

The next day I walked down into the city center. It was over a mile and a half of roads and streets, all sloping downwards, with me glancing back frequently so I could be sure of the hike back. The city center was comforting to me, shops and banks and areas with green grass and flowers, benches at strategic places, a long street perpendicular to the main street leading down to the station, more shops and pubs there, places to explore. Everything seemed so clean and fresh and neat and busy. The cadence of the people talking as they walked relaxed me. I discovered I was on a street called the Nethergate and I was directed to my right, told it was a short walk to the university, to stay on the road and not go on to the Hawkhill because that would take me to the back of the university.

There must be a particular quiet sort of emotional joy at being among many people in a totally new place, being a stranger, all troubles and fears left behind. I felt that way that day, somehow pleased with myself though all I'd done was get myself freshly cleaned and walked down streets to face my new future. It was my first time to feel that way and I've had many since but that time is

111

Survivor

deep in my memories, helped build my confidence, gave me a love of Dundee that has always been with me.

The bruise around my eye had faded to a quite presentable appearance, the cut in my lip almost closed, the place I'd lost the tooth not hurting at all. I always healed fast. My scars and acne I'd learned to live with. The thought of a crippled child walking was my defense and bulwark against any resurgence of misery about how I looked. So it was with happiness and confidence I walked up the Nethergate toward the university. It only took about ten minutes and even before I saw the tall tower of the administration building on my right I found a bookstore, stacks of new and used textbooks on display. I stopped there for a while, soaking in a feeling of adventure, a wanting sort of feeling, a desire to read and learn, not aware of the passage of time, engrossed in the pages I turned.

Although it was the weekend before term was to begin there were many students on the faculty grounds. I talked with some of them as I wandered and realized it was a cosmopolitan campus. Most of the students were Scots but there were many from England and India and Pakistan and Africa. I even met a lad from Iceland. I looked at the outside of the chemistry and physics buildings but didn't go inside. They were handsome large grey stone buildings with three levels of windows. Some students took me with them into the Student Union building where I was awed at the interior architecture of polished wood and moldings and plaques on the walls. It all gave me an overall impression of grandeur. It awakened in me the emotions I'd had cycling down the coast of Mayo, a pride in the origins of my family, Celtic pride, history on my side.

On Saturday evening there was a scheduled meeting in a large hall for all bejants and bejantines. It was crowded, with stalls for societies along the walls, a clamor of talking, students pushing past each other, laughter and excitement. I hadn't put on my suit jacket but I still wore a tie with my white shirt, taking my cue from the students I'd met on campus. I soon found out that it was an occasion for a university tradition. It was where a final year student would find a first year student to 'take on', basically adopt, in order to guide him or her through the first years. There were traditional obligations on each side. A Senior man would have a bejant. A

112

Senior woman would have a bejantine. It wasn't long before I had a Senior man. His name was Steve and he was a Londoner and a final year medical student. He had three friends who were looking for their own bejants and when that was done all eight of us left and started walking down the Nethergate. Steve explained to me that traditionally the Senior man would pay for everything that night, food and drinks, anything the bejant wanted. Later in the term there would be a day when my Senior man could call on me, even coming into class, demanding that I recite the Gaudeamus Igitur. If I couldn't do it I'd be obliged to give him a bottle of wine. My Senior man would always be there for me if I needed advice or guidance or got into trouble.

When we reached a large pub on the Nethergate I already knew I'd have to drink a beer. I managed to quench my reluctance, joining in the celebration as we found a table for us all to sit around. The pub was crowded with students, pints of beer on tables, a hubbub of conversation and introductions, a general air of festivity. In that atmosphere I became a beer drinker. Pint after pint of beer was brought to the table, the Senior men competing with each other, boasting that their particular bejant was keeping up, could handle his beer. I wanted to please Steve and threw all caution aside. I got drunk. Later that evening they took me in a taxi to my lodging, where they dumped my stumbling, apologizing body on my landlady. She didn't seem at all bothered, laughing in a pleased sort of way as though she was used to it, telling Steve she'd take care of me. The entire next day I spent in bed, suffering, being fussed over by my landlady.

My first chemistry class must have had about fifty or sixty students, sitting on long wooden polished benches with a backrest and a writing surface in front of us. There were wooden stairs on each side since we were ranked as if in an auditorium. It was all quite grand. I was surprised to hear many English accents around me, most upper class, even some I thought were aristocratic, unable to get into Oxford or Cambridge, not having the advantage of my three years in I.C.I, probably hopeless in a laboratory. Throughout that day, going to Mathematics class, going to Physics class, finding the schedule for our laboratory classes, I made three friends

Survivor

who were to be my closest friends during my university years. Ted Wakeling was from a farming family in Rutland; the smallest county in England. Brian Stockdale was from a farming family near Carlisle, just south of the Scottish border in North West England, and Dorothy Hughes from Bolton, near Manchester. She was a working class ici lass, from I.C.I. Dyestuffs Division in Lancashire. I liked Dorothy immediately. We had so much in common. Ted and Brian and talk of farms I could identify with. We would be close because all our classes would be the same, studying only the three subjects of chemistry, physics and mathematics.

During the day I was happy. At night was a different matter. I'd begun to have panic nightmares, waking in the middle of the night, fading images of my father coming after me, attacking me, taking me out of university, losing my bursary, dragging me back to Derby Street, battering my mother and Patricia for encouraging me. It happened so often I got into the habit of drinking several pints of beer in the Student Union before fiercely hiking up the streets to my lodging, attempting to exhaust myself so that I could get a good sleep. It worked sometimes.

It was on one of those evenings in the Student Union, in the basement pub, I made some more friends. They were Social Science students, bejants and second year, studying Politics, Philosophy and Economics. It happened in a chance way. I was invited to join a darts match by a tall blond lad who was playing 501 doubles and needed a partner. That involves starting with 501 points, getting a double to start, each member of a pair taking turns to decrease points, then finishing on an exact double, forfeiting score if the double is not reached. The blond lad let me go first and shouted out in glee as I started with a double twenty and then a triple twenty. We scored fast and he finished with the double. He asked me where I had learned to play darts like that and bought me a pint of beer. So darts sessions and pints of beer became a regular evening routine.

One night while about five teams were competing, a bejant began to complain that he had a paper to write about a social science topic. There was plenty of time between turns so I offered to read that part of his book and dictate his paper, explaining I was

114

Survivor

a very fast reader. It was an easy enough thing to do and by the end of the evening he had my dictation completed.

A few days later my reputation had spread since he'd got a good grade for the paper. It got me a lot of free beers. It got me a lot of requests. It also led me on to buy the book by Bertrand Russell titled 'A History of Western Philosophy' That drew me into buying more books he'd written and deciding I always wanted those books to go back to, to read sections often. Those students also introduced me to 'The Age Of Reason', by Jean-Paul Sartre, and from there on to reading books by Camus and Gide. So from a simple darts game I had been introduced to a new wonderland of reading, becoming educated. By then I'd lost my reluctance to read psychology and actually found it quite interesting, though economics I found to be too dry and politics just an amalgam of history and newspapers that I'd been reading since my newspaper delivering days.

I gave up looking for my own Hephaestion very early on. I didn't find any oblique hints from others, even when drinking beer, and I was fully aware that even in Scotland I was still under that English law that branded me a criminal if I ever even tried, and that loomed in my consciousness. So I was careful and circumspect and thought to myself that even if the remote possibility came about that I'd encounter someone who might be my own Hephaestion he would recoil in horror on seeing my face. I would have to soldier on alone.

The main student cafeteria was on the upper floor of an ultra modern building behind the academic buildings. It was on a large open piece of ground. The lower floor was used for sports facilities and had conventional brick walls. The upper floor was mainly floor to ceiling windows and could accommodate hundreds of students at round tables and chairs throughout the polished light oak hardwood floor. On Saturday nights the tables and chairs were moved so there was a large dance floor and room for a band. It was the beginning of the popular music era and though I was already familiar with music on Radio Luxembourg and had heard the music of Cliff Richard and Gerry and the Pacemakers, Billy Kramer and the Dakotas, Brian Poole and the Tremeloes, and had heard the first

115

Survivor

music by the Beatles, I had never been to a dance and was thrilled to hear the pounding music coming from the building as I and my new friends walked toward the sound. Dorothy was very knowledgeable, with experience of going to dances in Liverpool and her enthusiasm infected Ted and Brian and me as we joined the throng of our fellow students showing our tickets at the door. We'd made sure we'd drunk enough beer in the Student Union and had bought our tickets there. I became an enthusiast for going to 'hops' after that night. It was where I could dance and rejoice in movement, letting my emotions surge from me, shutting out all but the music. There were many local bands playing the music at the top of the charts.

Little did we know that we were at the beginning of the sixties popular music scene. The Beatles had only recently reached the top of the charts. I found I was a good dancer and within weeks became popular with Dorothy and other girls, pulled out on the dance floor, so it got to the point where I'd spend the entire night dancing, realizing early on that I shouldn't spend too much time with any one girl, seeing the revelry and giggling and cuddling outside the building as the night finished. I didn't want a repeat of what I'd gone through with Diana. I didn't want to encourage any girl to like me too much. Eventually I'd leave before the end of the night, saying I had a long walk back to my lodging. It did spread my popularity and that was an invigorating feeling. I was going through many changes and in trying to distance myself from my memories, I began to tell a different history of myself to protect myself from breaking down in conversation.

I'd had no problem in the Bursar's office putting down my home town as Roscommon, Ireland, for university records, for that was the truth in my heart. But in my first drunken evening with my Senior man and his friends I almost broke down into tears and despair when they began to ask me about parents and family. I quickly diverted my emotions and told them my parents had died when I was young and I'd been raised by my Uncle Ken and my Aunt Maureen while going to St. Mary's College. They had come back from Africa the previous year with my little cousin Susan and had bought an imposing house on the upper level of Yarm Road,

116

Survivor

near Ropner Park. I'd always wished they were my parents and just by shifting their return from Africa to eight years earlier I was able to talk about them and not be overwhelmed with tears.

Another change came in a suggestion from Ted Wakeling. He asked me wasn't it more correct to call me Sean rather than John since I was from Ireland. I readily agreed with him pointing out that on paper I'd still be John and that if they wanted to write my name the Irish way I'd expect it to be written with an accent as in Seán, which was proper. So in that way Ted and Brian and Dorothy began to call me Sean, and that became my nickname, and all my new friends called me that, my distance from my memories of Derby Street cementing it into place. That has been my nickname since though I still put the accent in the name when I write it, keeping John for official documents.

I was noticed one day leaving my chemistry laboratory class early. The laboratory was supervised by an elderly lady, Dr. Kathleen Watson. I'd got into the habit of arriving for the three hour lab before the other students and organizing myself, just as I'd done in I.C.I., and could usually complete the assignment in an hour and a half, heading down to the Student Union for the rest of the afternoon. Dr. Watson stopped me from leaving the room and made me go back and repeat the experiment, watching every move I made. She questioned me while I worked and found out I'd worked in I.C.I. for three years. Over the next month I could feel her watching me. She'd given the class the task of differential crystallization of racemic amidine, a mix of optical isomers, made in her research laboratory across the hallway. I put all my attention into that, scrupulously cleaning the beakers and using fine filter papers to strain the hot solution, then leaving the solution to cool undisturbed and covered for a week, just as Mr. Rudd had taught me. It was a success. I'd produced a large single crystal of one of the optical isomers. Dr. Watson was delighted, bringing in a photographer to take a picture of the crystal, my classmates crowding around while I attempted to be modest.

After that day she told me I didn't need to take the assigned laboratories but could work with her on her research. So for the rest of my university days I worked on her research. It did lead on to a

117

Survivor

publication in the Journal of The Chemical Society in which she put my name first, published shortly after I arrived in America.

I've often wondered what it must be like to grow up in a loving family, where life is clearly defined, when the effects of setbacks and disasters are compensated for with warmth and safety, with always a security to retreat to, a room to identify as home. For me I had to search for all those things, looking to sympathetic relatives, to kind strangers, and always knowing it was a substitute for what could have been. I liked to hear talk of family life from my fellow students, hungry for any scraps of comfort I might get from them, imagining myself to have such safety, though in truth I only knew of such things from when I was very young in Ballybohan, hanging on to the front gate waiting for my grandfather to come around the turn on the boreen road.

At times, later in life, I've tried to urge others to reflect on their good fortune of having naturally what I had to search for, but not often, since I've usually found only incomprehension, an inability to feel how lonely I felt in the days I was trying to do my best. Of course my loneliness was compounded with my perception that the heroic love I sought was lost in the dust of history, that I had to hide my feelings for fear of going to jail, and that I had to stride forward with a damaged face, tackling each problem as it arose, trying not to look back.

My Scots landlady gave me some of what I so badly needed and in turn I spent time talking with her and listening to her, always up on my feet to help her, to be there for her. She bought tomatoes, expensive there in those days, to slice onto my morning toast. I appreciated that, feeling love for me. She would show her concern for me and I would wish I could do more for her. So in that sense I was able to find some idea of what my fellow students felt when talking of their families.

On Friday November 22, 1963 we spent an entire evening together. I was in my bedroom getting ready to join my friends down in the Student Union when my landlady came in with a state of agitation. The American President had been killed in an assassination. BBC news was transmitting continuous coverage. We sat and watched until BBC ended its evening program with the

Survivor

national anthem. We didn't know that much about America but the tragedy of such a horrible thing brought sadness about the world into our conversation that night. My landlady went to bed as the national anthem went on and told me to switch the television off when I went to bed. I was about to do that, the screen flickering with dots and streaks of static when I heard a speech coming from the television. It was a call to support the Scottish National Party, coming illegally from a fishing boat in the North Sea, and I listened through to the end. I went to bed that night with wild imaginings, that this time of the assassination of the American President was seen as an opportunity for the Scots to rise up against the English. I made sure my Irish passport was within my reach. I was ready to support the Scots if there was a revolution.

The next day as I reached the Student Union the assassination of President Kennedy was the talk of everyone, the newspaper headlines blazing with it. The days passed. There was no revolution.

I'd written to my Aunt Maureen to ask if I could visit during the Christmas vacation and she wrote back and told me I could. I'd got a job for the end of term working for Dundee Post Office at their sorting center for the Christmas rush and that would be until the end of Christmas Day. That satisfied me. I liked that in Scotland that day was a regular working day. I had as many hours as I could work and did several double shifts, keeping thoughts of Derby Street away from me. On the train south to Edinburgh then Newcastle and on to Stockton I reflected on how much my life had changed in just three months. I looked forward to seeing my Uncle Ken and Aunt Maureen. My uncle was an amazing man to me. When he had gone to work at the Williamson's Diamond Mine in Africa as an engineer he had shown me that change was possible. He had gone out beyond the perimeter fence of the mine with a recorder and cine camera and made friends with the tribes in the area. He had been made an honorary African chief. He was a man without prejudice. My aunt Maureen had trained as a nurse and when one day a man from beyond the perimeter fence was brought in badly mauled by a lion nobody wanted to attend to him because he was a leper. Maureen bound his wounds. He had lost a lot of

119

Survivor

blood. There was no transfusion equipment. Maureen knew she had a universal blood group. She took a long rubber tube and put hypodermic needles in each end and stood above the leper on the floor and pumped her arm and her own blood into the dying man. He lived. When Ken and Maureen were the last Europeans working at the mine they were given two jeep loads of presents, ivories, skins, carvings, which they brought back to England and into the house they bought on Yarm Road.

I enjoyed my visit there. They cooked together, teaching me how to cook Indian curries from the authentic spices, another thing they had learned at the mine, and spoke in words of Swahili, telling me about Africa. I loved them very much.

I sold my bike when I was there to a young lad for five pounds.

Just the day before I was to return to Dundee a telephone call came from my landlady's niece. My landlady had died. On returning to Dundee I had to get a place to live. I had to get another lodging to live in. That was much nearer to the university but it was not as good as the old Scots lady who had concern for me. I was just a lodger, expected to speak in French to the mother's three young children at breakfast. I found no warmth there.

So in that way I came to the end of my academic year and prepared to return to I.C.I. for the summer, going to Ken and Maureen's house where they had a bedroom prepared for me.

I'd been writing to my grandmother in Ireland and to my Aunt Josie so I did know there was protection for me. They assured me my father didn't know where I was or where I'd gone and they wouldn't let him know. They didn't tell my mother either, presuming he'd beat it out of her, but they did tell her I was alright and not to worry about me. They had no news of Patricia, or Mary, or my brothers Tommy and Terry. Billy was still my sister's boyfriend and that gave me comfort.

When I'd left I.C.I. the previous September my salary had risen to thirty five pounds a month with thirty pounds five shillings and sixpence into my bank account. When I returned for the summer of 1964 I was given a special project developing chromatography for the side products of the urea plant and my

120

Survivor

salary by August had risen to over forty three pounds a month with forty pounds four shillings and sixpence deposited into my bank. I felt wealthy.

When I returned to Dundee at the end of September I'd been informed by letter from the university accommodations officer that due to my requirements to avoid sugar and salt I was to be given a furnished flat on Airlie Place and had to get two friends to move in and share the rent. Ted and Brian were delighted to share with me. Airlie Place was right inside the university and it was difficult for second year students to get a flat there. I'd also decided my two second year subjects would be Chemistry and Biochemistry. I'd already decided on a future of study in Organic Chemistry and related fields. I would miss Physics but not Mathematics. I could only take classes in two subjects since the second year would show merit to be accepted into an Honours program of two years studying only one subject. Failing acceptance would mean taking a final year of two other subjects to get an ordinary B.Sc., good enough but I'd set my sights higher.

My second year developed into a continuous party atmosphere. I went to all the hops, was invited to many parties, and went out drinking every night. I missed a lot of classes but kept up with research in Dr. Watson's laboratory and kept catching up with my studies by getting lecture notes from Ted and Dorothy. I'd shared some of my feelings with Ted and Brian and Dorothy, not talking of my own Hephaestion but putting it into cruder terms of sex as they did, that being more acceptable in the environment I found myself in. I had terrible feelings of loneliness and abandonment and sexual frustrations. I took risks when drunk but that came to nothing. Being popular had an awful price. I never shared with anyone my feelings of being so alone. I partied, I drank, I laughed and joked, I danced. I could think of no other way to live my life. I could find no way to solve my loneliness. Finding my own Hephaestion seemed even more remote than ever. I was taking risks that could put me into jail. Even my love for chemistry could not fill that void in me. I stayed in Dundee for the Christmas vacation, working at the Post Office Sorting Center, even for two days being taken out on the collecting vans. There was a lot of

121

snow that winter and it was quite an adventure going out to remote villages, being given a dram of whiskey to speed us on our way.

I made many friends that year and got to know even more. I regret that I did not get to know them better and kept in touch with them because I liked them and had a good time in their company. I wish they could know that. It was my inhibitions that stopped me from taking friendships further, the fear that they would end the friendship if they were to know how different I was from them, that I did not share their romantic interests, their desires. I was always afraid of the society around me. I didn't know why they would turn against me but I read the newspapers and I read the magazines. The previous year I'd dared to go alone in broad daylight to a cinema playing the film Victim, about unrequited love of a young man for an older man, and blackmail and jail and suicide. It was a controversial film. It showed me a world of cruelty and intolerance. I knew the mocking derisive words. I knew the pain and hurt they caused me. And I was so alone.

As the early months of 1965 gave way to milder weather it seemed as if the whole world was awakening. The Aldermaston March, the campaign for nuclear disarmament, was planned for Easter in London. We were preparing for Rag Week: a week in which students would dress in outrageous costumes and put on stunts and sell a booklet of jokes and cartoons. It was all to raise money for various charities and for that week it was a riot of color and student enthusiasm. I put down my name to join the groups going with collecting cans to the pubs and clubs in the poorer sections of Dundee. I'd had the experience of the previous year in which patrons of the higher class of clubs and pubs would barely tolerate our antics, putting only low coinage into the cans, but in the rough working class pubs we were welcomed with shouts of encouragement and the cans soon filled with shillings and half crowns, sometimes even ten shilling notes and pound notes from people who seemed as if they could barely afford it. I'd become used to the fact that each Scottish bank issued its own design pound note with the different colors and designs contrasting with the English pound. We knew that although the value was the same

Survivor

many shops in England wouldn't accept a Scottish pound note. That would make us even more likely to try it on going to England.

The music and the dancing at the hops seemed to be a new age beginning. The Beatles and The Rolling Stones were most popular. The Kinks and The Byrds and The Moody Blues and The Animals and The Hollies and The Seekers all flooded us with new thoughts and ideas and defiance of conventional authority. It was an exciting time and a wonder that any of us got any studying done. I bought a second hand reel to reel tape recorder, a great bulky thing, and began making tapes from other student's record players and singles collections. I became even more popular taking my tape recorder to parties. I began to collect the music of Bob Dylan. I was neglecting my studies.

I was twenty one on March 4. Ted and Brian and I planned a spectacular party in our flat. The invitations were written on parchment and tied with a red ribbon and placed inside sparkling clean pint milk bottles we had been collecting for the occasion, the glass and tied parchment being unique and seen throughout the day as we distributed invitations. We stacked all the furniture into the smallest room and used the other two rooms for dancing and mingling. One room was for popular music from my tape recorder, another room was for sitar music by some Indian friends, the room with stacked furniture and the kitchen was for folk singing. There were casks of beer and guests were expected to bring more. I had a huge poster on the wall where guests signed their names. I still have that poster to this day. That night was even more successful than we expected. We had to put doormen to restrict entry. The flight of stairs was crowded with students who hadn't got invitations trying to get in. There was well over a hundred people at one time in the flat, music blasting, sitar music, folk singing, everyone having a good time. The two old ladies in the flat next door had invited in friends that night after we took over four bottles of wine that afternoon and told them to come over and tell us if it got too loud. They never did come over. The next day was a Friday and the old ladies told us their friends had enjoyed the excitement. It was one of the best parties of that year. It did attract a lot of attention and talk.

123

Survivor

My research work for Dr. Watson was going well. I'd developed a technique for a condensation of the optically active amidine with itself, forming first a symmetrical dihydrotetrazine, which would become oxidized by exposure to air to the corresponding tetrazine, aromatic molecules analogous to the benzene molecule but with four nitrogen atoms in the ring. I was working on a way to isolate the dihydrotetrazine before oxidation. I had a great joy in working in that laboratory. I'd learned from Mr.Redman how to focus on the laboratory bench, shutting away the world outside, learning from him how to shut out thoughts of Derby Street and my father. Dr. Watson was pleased with me and would comment in surprise at some of the simple techniques I used.

At times I felt as though I was solving all the problems in my life but then reality would bring me back to ground. I was still in peril that my father would find out where I was and expose Josie's subterfuge with my mother, signing the Durham County Council Bursary application twice a year. I knew he could wreck that and stop my bursary. I was still afraid that the risks I took when drunk would put me into jail. I could think no further than finishing my degree. I was devastated when I took my Chemistry and Biochemistry exams in early June and failed. I had one more chance to retake the exams at the end of the summer. That sobered me up. I returned to I.C.I. and was given another job when I told them I needed to earn a lot of money. I was placed on a shift system, going around the research site checking and recording data from other people's experiments. I'd work from ten at night to seven in the morning for three days, take twenty four hours off then from seven in the morning to four in the afternoon for three days, another twenty four hours off, then four in the afternoon to ten at night to get three days off before starting the shift cycle again. That disrupted any urge I had to go to the pubs. It also earned me a lot of money.

I got myself lodging a short walk from the research buildings. I'll never forget Mr. and Mrs. Stephenson. They were in their early sixties and had been 'in service' to a manor house of a Lord when younger. Changing times led to Mr. Stephenson getting a job in the I.C.I. manufacturing plant, his wife keeping their home and

124

Survivor

cooking. She was a stupendous cook, the best meals I'd ever had, and the girth of she and her husband testified to that. I'd explained to them that I only wanted to work and study for the summer, getting ready for examinations. They took me in and were incredibly kind to me. When I'd come in late in the evening after the library closed they would have gone to bed early but there would be a damp tablecloth over a dining room table covered in apple pies and cheeses and ham slices and bread and pickles, with tea leaves in a pot by the kitchen stove, ready for me to heat water. I couldn't see possibly how they could be making any money from me with all the food I was fed and wanted to give more but they wouldn't take it. Mrs. Stephenson would do my laundry and even iron my underwear. One night I confided in them what my life had been like in Stockton and how afraid I was of my father. Later that night, through closed doors, I heard Mr. Stephenson talking to his wife, his deep slow heavy Durham accent catching my attention, "if that man comes looking for that lad I'll break his arms and legs. I'll not let him get in." I had no doubt that Mr. Stephenson would defend me. I loved them both.

At the end of the summer I returned to my flat in Airlie place and did so well in my repeat exams that I was offered an Honours place in both the Chemistry department and the Biochemistry department. I was in. I chose Chemistry. All I had to do was study chemistry for two years and then take my final Honours examinations. However Brian and Ted had to move out. They'd only been given one year. They moved to a flat in a tenement building near the university. I invited two students I barely knew to join me. One was Christopher Jones, a Protestant, son of a British civil servant from Northern Ireland. The other was Girish Chande, son of a wealthy mill owner in Kenya. I intended to be like my Uncle Ken, without prejudice, accepting to all people. It was a good decision. I still remained close friends with Ted and Brian and Dorothy and we continued to go to hops and drinking together.

I'd selected classes in various fields of organic chemistry and was developing a fascination with the molecular interactions of biological systems. I could see whole continents of knowledge for me to learn. The first three dimensional X-rays of enzymes were

Survivor

being published. It was as if that and dancing and drinking occupied all of my attention. I still read newspapers but with the Labour Party running the government, and Harold Wilson as Prime Minister, events occurring in the British Isles and abroad were peripheral to the interests of all of us.

Only one event galvanized the student community. That was when the Rhodesian National Front with Ian Smith as their Prime Minister won a landslide election victory in Rhodesia near the end of the first week of May. We were outraged. Apartheid in South Africa was bad enough. We had long since refused to buy South African fruit. But this defiance toward the government had student demonstrations demanding the Harold Wilson take immediate military action. It was a rational thing to us that while the world was getting better this horrible step back into ignorance should be stopped, by force. We didn't get what we wanted but it did begin political forces that eventually toppled Ian Smith and his government. It took too long.

The end of the academic year came and I returned for the summer to I.C.I. to live again with Mr. and Mrs. Stephenson. Junior Honours year students didn't have examinations so there was no pressure on me and I was able to go back into a regular working day. I was given a project and an assistant to work out the kinetics of hydrolysis of by products in the Vinyl Acetate plant. It involved learning new techniques of sealing solutions in thick glass tubes under pressure, varying the temperature in a water tank, and then cooling the tubes with ice, snapping the top and doing titration analysis on the contents. I'd completed several courses on kinetics by that time and was able to demonstrate that steady state kinetics were controlling hydrolysis for some of the molecules. At the end of the summer when I presented all the evidence and graphs to my boss, Dr. Peter Horn, he was very happy with me and told me my work was going to be an official I.C.I. report and that he was going to hire a full time person to continue my work.

I'd put enough money into my bank account to plan for a vacation before returning to Dundee. I'd have two weeks and I'd planned an ambitious hitchhike trip across Europe with the objective of reaching Yugoslavia. I'd bought a rucksack and joined

Survivor

the International Youth Hostel organization, planning on staying in Youth Hostels. I wanted to meet different people and hear different languages and experience different cultures. I wanted to expand my awareness of the world. I wanted to see it for myself. I had a barely suppressed haunting thought that if I was to travel among others further afield I might one day see another lad looking at me and see in his eyes that he was my own Hephaestion and we'd talk of Achilles and Patroclus and begin our life together. I took a train to London then a student flight to Amsterdam. I spent two days there. The Youth Hostel closed its doors by ten o'clock at night but I was fine with that. I ate in the three floor student cafeteria just off the Dam Square. A single ticket, my student ID, and I could eat as much as I wanted from different cuisines, including Indonesian. I walked the Leidsestraat and Leidseplein and went to the Rikjsmuseum. I went to the red light district and back down the Damrak. I wandered up and down the canals. I was so awed by the Rikjsmuseum I went back a second day and wandered in the museum for hours wishing I knew more about art. I enjoyed everything. I liked the profusion of flowers for sale on the streets, eating fried potatoes with cheese from open stalls, smelling the aroma of cigar smoke walking back up the Leidsestraat.

From Amsterdam I hitchhiked to Germany and down to Aachen where I booked into the Youth Hostel there. That was quite an experience. It was a huge modern construction of wood and glass, astonishingly clean, hundreds of young people of all ages. In youth hostelling the rules include keeping certain hours, having a thin cotton 'sleeping bag', more a sort of sheets sewn together with a pocket for a pillow, to sleep in yet protect the mattress and blankets and pillows supplied with the bunk beds in dormitories. Before leaving in the morning a 'duty' has to be done. That could involve cleaning windows, or washing floors, or polishing furniture. The duty has to be done before getting the Youth Hostel card given back.

The Aachen Youth Hostel gave me a unique experience. I awoke at six in the morning to the blast of loud bagpipe music and commands to get up. It was in several languages. It went on and on. With that din nobody could sleep on. When I got down to the front

127

Survivor

desk for my duty I was assigned to supervise about a dozen young kids, about ten years old, in some sort of German scouting uniform. I had to make sure they ate their breakfast and clean up after them, handing the dishes to an Italian lass doing her duty washing them in an industrial size dishwasher. I found the German people to be very friendly, the drivers who picked me up going out of their way to help me. So I hitchhiked out of Aachen and on to the autobahn south toward Munich. It was to be over 400 miles but I had seen how fast the cars were on the autobahn the day before and it was still early in the morning. I got several rides with only minutes between them but by early afternoon with almost two hundred miles yet to get Munich I got stuck for over an hour at an ingang to the autobahn with only an occasional passing driver waving apologetically and signaling that they were only local. I was sitting on my backpack when a police car drew up. The two policemen looked very authoritarian and didn't speak English. I managed to explain to them I was hitching to Munich and showed them my passport and Youth Hostel card. To my alarm they insisted I get into the back of the police car. For the next half hour I thought I was in trouble, not able to understand what they were saying to me. The car was travelling at a frightening speed. Suddenly they pulled over by the side of the autobahn at an ingang and indicated I should get out. The young policeman got out and pointed to a place at the top of the ingang. "Here", he said, "better. Hitchhike here." He then stood there and put out his thumb as if he was the hitchhiker. A car pulled up. The policeman talked to the driver. I had another ride. I was stunned and relieved and after I looked at my map later I found the police had taken me over fifty miles and the next driver took me another seventy miles. I arrived at the Munich Youth Hostel after a very adventurous day.

It was Okctoberfest time in Munich. I hadn't planned it. I was just lucky. I didn't know it was a beer drinking folk festival within walking distance of the Youth Hostel until the following morning when I joined a group of Germans and Italians at the front desk. I could hear the brass bands a half mile before we got to the fairground. There were huge tents like circus tents with long wooden tables and benches, a constant flow of serving women

128

Survivor

carrying liter steins of beer and the crowds of people on the benches linking arms and swaying to the music of the bands and roaring out German songs. My companions got us a place to sit and we joined in, as they tried to teach me some German words. We all began to laugh since I clearly couldn't make out a word even when it was shouted at me. Some of the serving women and the people on the benches were wearing traditional dress. It was a remarkable celebration. We were able to buy bratwurst and onions in long bread rolls. We stayed there all day and when we staggered back to the Youth Hostel later in the day I was carrying a stone stein with Munich etched on the side, given to me by an older couple on a nearby table who were enthusiastic about Ireland and Scotland.

The Oktoberfest goes on for sixteen days so I just had to go back the next day and finished up carrying back a liter stein of thick heavy glass given me some other people. I was really experiencing what I had set out to do.

The next day I got out onto the autobahn again. My next destination was Klagenfurt in Austria. That would be almost two hundred and twenty miles. It was a long day and took many rides but I finally arrived in the picturesque mountain town of Klagenfurt. The Youth Hostel sign was above a tourist office on the main street. I was relieved when the woman there spoke English. She told me that I was the only hosteller to be staying there that night and she took me out the door and pointed to an imposing castle type structure a short distance away and gave me a large ornate iron key. She suggested I go settle in and go back to her so she could take me shopping for food for dinner and breakfast. We went for coffee at a table outside a restaurant as I explained I wanted to cross into Yugoslavia without a visa. She told me that would be impossible to hitch on the roads across the border and I might even get arrested or shot. She suggested I get a ticket for the train from Klagenfurt to Ljubljana, capital of Slovenia in northern Yugoslavia and make a fuss waving my Irish passport when the visa inspectors came along the train corridor at the border. She told me there would be a lot of papers to inspect because it would be a customs check as well and they didn't like to hold the train up too long. She also advised I buy a ticket that would take me out to the

129

coast at Rijeka to enjoy the beach. It was an active tourist town and I'd find people there to talk with.

I took her advice and it worked out well. The inspectors gave me a hard time for a while but they were busy so stamped my passport and moved on. As the train moved out into Slovenia the two middle aged housewives sitting opposite me, surrounded by numerous open carrier bags and packages were laughing and explaining to me in broken English and French that my diversion with the inspectors had helped them. They were smuggling the parts for a small washing machine back to their home in Ljubljana. So I entered Yugoslavia without a visa and helped housewives smuggle washing machine parts. That I felt was a good thing to do. I had reached the furthest point on my adventure.

Rijeka was beautiful with sunny weather. I got a place in a home with a family through the tourist office. They had two young girls about my own age and I relaxed with them on the beach for three days, eating with them and their mother at night, watching Russian television programs, talking about the world. The three of them spoke fairly good English and were educated. It opened me up to awareness of other cultures and ideas. One of the girls, Radomira Seka, took me to buy a liter of Yugoslav brandy and to the exchange to change my Yugoslav money into Italian money before getting the train from Rijeka to Trieste just up the coast.

After getting on the train and doing some calculations I discovered that due to devaluation while I was there I had left Yugoslavia with more money than I'd gone in with.

I stayed at the Youth Hostel in Trieste for several days. It was on the beach and outside town, the low white homes and buildings ascending up the hills in the sunshine was beautiful. I met two Australian girls at the hostel and we had fun exploring and hanging out on the beach. Italian I found much more understandable, reminding me of a mixture of Latin and French, while spoken conversation enchanted me and made me think I'd like to learn to speak Italian. My days were getting short so I reluctantly left Trieste and got out onto the road to Venice and on to Milan. I didn't have time for those cities so just kept hitching on up to the border with France.

Survivor

I didn't like hitching in France. It was difficult and the one Youth Hostel I stayed in was old and run down. By the time I got to northern France I had a stroke of luck. I was picked up by a young English aristocrat driving a sports car. He was heading to the car-air ferry at Dieppe and was not only crossing to England but driving on up to Edinburgh to stay with friends. He had been to the Oktoberfest. He clearly was quite wealthy. His name was Nick Ayr and he had Ayr on the license plate of his car. As I was telling him of the adventures I had gone through he insisted I stay with him at a motel in Dieppe and have dinner with him at his favorite restaurant there. We could then cross to England the following day refreshed and drive on up to just north of Edinburgh where his friends lived. He was a gentleman and I enjoyed his company. When he dropped me off north of the Firth of Forth the next day it only took me a few hours to hitch up to Perth and east to Dundee.

Survivor

Chapter 8

October 1966 brought me into a phase of life where I felt terribly old. It had been my twenty second birthday the previous March, not celebrated like the year before, just drinking with my close friends. My hand and head tremors were bothering me. It seemed as if any kind of stress would set them off. Christopher Jones and Girish Chande were not as close in friendship as Ted and Brian and Dorothy and so parties in our flat was not even brought up. I had lots of invitations to parties from other students and I went to just about all of them. I'd returned to Dundee for my fourth and Senior Honours year in a state of indecision about where my life was leading. I'd moved into a room in Belmont Tower, on the ninth floor, a residence hall in the center of the university grounds, and I had a magnificent view of the Tay River with seals sunning themselves on sandbanks in the middle of the river at low tide. It was a compact place for me to reflect and try to work out how to find a way ahead.

My age was weighing on me. So many of the people I knew seemed confident about their future prospects. I didn't feel that way. My major problem was about to come to a conclusion. My Aunt Josie and my mother would soon be signing the final application for my Bursary in the coming January. That would rid me of the persistent fear that my father would find out and wreck my university days. Even my panic nightmares were losing their hold on me. I'd wake up and put all the lights on and read, waiting for dawn, knowing that as light came into the sky I'd regain my confidence and determination. My major problem now became a source of distress, that my hands and head would tremor at times of stress. It was common knowledge when I was growing up that the family carried a mild form of Parkinson's disease. My grandmother in Ballybohan had it. Other people in the family had tremors. My attitude to that was that I could quench it in the evenings with a couple of pints of beer, I didn't really expect to live that long anyway, so I intended to live life to the fullest, burning the candle on both ends as is commonly said. The music of the Beatles and the Rolling Stones, the dancing which I loved and went to hops and

132

Survivor

other dances at every chance I could, the parties, the revelry, I embraced as if there wasn't much time left. I wondered at times if that was a consequence of my age, if my friends felt the same way, but I never asked, thinking I'd have to bring in my search for my own Hephaestion, even doubting myself on that, thinking of it as a foolish part of my younger days. There was still of course my damaged face but I had the thought of a crippled child to protect me, and I'd developed a hope that future medical advances would smooth out my scars.

Whether it was foolish or not I decided to myself that when I was sure my January Bursary was secure in the bank I'd continue my search for love. Belmont Residence Hall was the Tower block I was in, along with two extensions of student rooms on two floors. There was a dining hall for all meals. There was a billiards room and a television room and a mail area where I had my own slot to receive letters. There were over a hundred and twenty students in Belmont. My room had a very large window and a wash basin. There were ten rooms on the floor. There was a small kitchen and toilets and bathroom at the end of the floor. It was a very modern building. The lift, or as I learned later to call an elevator, taking me down to the dining hall level, was clean and efficient. I felt it was an ideal place to meet a lot of my fellow students, increase the numbers as it were, to take the risk in drunken conversations to hint and even bluntly talk of what I was looking for. If I was accused and arrested I could talk my way out of it. My English friend Alan Cook the previous year had been arrested for pissing against a wall in public. When his legal representative presented evidence with witnesses that Alan had indeed been drunk the case was dismissed. That was when I found out that the laws of Scotland were more humane than England. Also more interesting in that instead of just guilty and not guilty Scots law provided for a verdict of not proven. Armed with that knowledge I reasoned that bolder drunken talk might lead me to love and the consequences of going to jail would not be likely. After all if you couldn't be legally guilty of a crime for pissing against a wall in public while drunk then surely I wouldn't be legally guilty of a crime for talking of loving another man while drunk.

Survivor

My research work in Dr. Watson's laboratory was coming to a conclusion. I'd been able to synthesise and separate gram quantities of the optically active dihydrotetrazine and tetrazine. I'd taken infrared and ultraviolet spectra. The technician running nuclear magnetic resonance scans had given me the charts. Quantitative analysis from a commercial firm had added to the proof of structure. She had sent samples to the University of London for Circular Dichroism and Optical Rotatory Dispersion studies. I'd been careful. I knew my samples were pure. Dr. Watson began to talk of me doing research after I graduated. She talked of me doing a doctorate, maybe even at Cambridge. That gave me a sense of disbelief that they would accept someone like me but she was sure of it, telling me I had the skills.

That term went by quickly. When the winter break came in I had to move out of Belmont for two weeks. Ted and Brian gave me the key to their tenement flat. They were going home. I had it to myself. I began working at the Dundee Post Office sorting center. It was familiar to me by then and it would be a welcome source of money. I'd run short and was being very frugal, counting the days until the Post Office would pay me. That would be the day after Christmas day. It was a cold winter with a lot of snow. It was a couple of miles to the job. There was a hole on one of my leather shoes. I was back to the days of cardboard inserts. The flat was cold. I made a bed for myself on the kitchen floor. I kept the gas stove oven on while I was there, making sure I had plenty of shillings to feed the gas meter. It might sound miserable to some but I was content. When I finished work on Christmas Day I had a dinner of baked beans on buttered toast and settled in for the night with a stack of used science fiction magazines. I knew I only had to make it through to June.

As the snow melted and I returned to Belmont Hall, cashed my hundred pound Bursary, and met with all my friends, I was rejuvenated. I talked with Ted and Brian honestly about my feelings and how hard it was for me to have to put up a front all the time. They weren't surprised, telling me they had guessed years before it was more than I'd told them, knowing it was more than just sex with me, especially not having a girlfriend since I was so popular

134

Survivor

and many girls had tried to start a relationship with me, especially girls from the Art College next to the university. I'd been going to their dances and knew a lot of Scots girls. Ted was particularly considerate, telling me it made no difference to him, told me to 'go for it' because everyone should have someone to love them. He had a girlfriend he was planning to marry and somehow his acceptance and encouragement gave me a relief, as though I was sighing deep inside me.

I made a lot of new friends in Belmont Hall. One of them lived on my floor. His name was Glenn Taylor. He was from Glasgow and a second year student. I'd already tried my new strategy of holding bold drunken talk with three other students and been rejected, not on the night of the drunkenness, but on the following days and after, ignoring me, withdrawing friendship, cold terse words when I tried to initiate conversation. So with Glenn I didn't take that step. I enjoyed his company. I liked the easy way he talked about his mother and brother and family life in Glasgow. He was tall and attractive with a wry sense of humor and he would tease me when he thought I was being too serious. It wasn't until my twenty third birthday when he gave me a birthday card that I took the next step. I wasn't drunk. It was a Saturday and an unusually warm day for that time of the year and he had the window in his room wide open. I poured out my heart to him about my life in Derby Street and my fears and wanting so much for someone to love me. He didn't interrupt me, letting me talk on and on, tears coming from my eyes at times. I felt sympathy coming from him, calmness, letting me finish. He then got up off his bed and motioned for me to stand up from my chair and gave me a long hug and during that said quietly: "you know I'm not that way," still holding me, letting me know he was still my friend. I was drained from the emotional outburst. He then said: "so you are gay?". I told him I knew the word but I didn't find anything merry about it. He laughed and told me one of his good friends in Glasgow was gay and used to go to Amsterdam on holidays to meet other gay people.

That afternoon was a turning point in my life. Glenn told me he'd go to Amsterdam with me at the end of term and he'd go with

135

Survivor

me to the gay clubs even if it wasn't his cup of tea and he'd help me find love.

The next few months were hectic. I was applying for work at several companies. I knew I could still go back to I.C.I. if I wasn't sucessful. Dr. Watson was still taking to me about Cambridge and a doctorate, and Glenn and I were making our plans to go to Amsterdam. I partied too much and I got drunk too much. It was as if I wanted to have a grand conclusion to my university life.

We were to get a student flight from London to Amsterdam and had booked a week in a student hotel near the Leidseplein. I was excited about the trip. I talked to Glenn about the Rijksmuseum and the red light district and the canals and the flowers everywhere and the student cafeteria and he'd laugh and remind me of the gay clubs we'd go to in the evening. His friend had given him the names and I was surprised to find they were in the Leidseplein and in streets off the Leidsestraat. I'd been anticipating hidden places in disreputable areas.

I had several interviews set up so I missed classes going on train journeys down to London. The best offer I got was work in a research laboratory investigating potential veterinary drugs. It was a division of the Welcome Foundation. It was in Berkhamsted, a pleasant country village about thirty three miles north of London. The president of the Division seemed more interested that my degree would be from St. Andrews University than anything else. I was offered a salary of one thousand two hundred pounds a year. Comparing with my classmates it was the highest offer anyone had received. I accepted the job, arranging to start just after my holiday in Amsterdam.

June came and final examinations and I was devastated to find that I had only got a third class Honours degree. That stopped any talk of Cambridge and a doctorate. I'd need at least an upper second for that. Ted got an upper second and Brian got a lower second. Other classmates were astonished by my result, telling me that everyone thought I'd get a first. I shrugged it off. I was only working class. That was good enough. I still had a great job. I decided that I wouldn't go to the graduation ceremony in June, mainly out of shame that I'd only got a third, but also the

136

Survivor

September graduation at St. Andrews in Fife was going to be the last for students from Dundee. That summer Dundee was going to become independent as Dundee University. It would be a distinction I could add to my accomplishments.

Glenn met up with me in Edinburgh station. He'd been home in Glasgow to have some time with his family. The train to London and the flight to Amsterdam aroused an excitement in me, that I was finally taking that step to meet other people like me. It still was a difficult thing to envisage, wondering if they would be men who repel me even though Glenn kept telling me that if they were like his friend in Glasgow they would be just ordinary people, not at all like the lurid descriptions I'd read in newspapers and magazines. I can suppose that in this modern age it is easy for a young man to assert his identity and find the right place to go to 'come out'. I was twenty three. I'd never met a gay person. I was exhilarated and afraid. I wondered if I could find my own Hephaestion. I was fortunate to have a good straight friend like Glenn to walk beside me into that world.

Now that we were in Amsterdam I had an internal conflict. I was both happy and apprehensive. Exploring the Rijksmuseum with Glenn was even better than my first time. He knew a lot about art and told me many things about the paintings and the painters and the history of Holland. We walked the canals and I showed him the places I'd been before. We ate in the student cafeteria and bought snacks in a sandwich automat on the Leidsestraat. We walked past the places his friend had written down for him. I didn't want to go in with daylight still in the sky. I wanted to wait until evening, until near sunset. I wanted to spend more hours laughing and joking and having Glenn's company before I took a step that I knew might be right or could be terribly wrong. We went for an evening meal at the student cafeteria and talked. I feared that the club would be just like what I'd read in newspapers and magazines, that I'd be repulsed, that my dream of finding love would be a fantasy. I was fully prepared to be disappointed. Glenn and I made an agreement that if either of us became uncomfortable we'd leave right away.

When we entered that first club my fears and apprehensions began to fade. It wasn't crowded at that time of the evening though

137

Survivor

it would be later. I looked around and it was just as if it was like a nice Irish pub except there were no women there. As we drank chilled Heineken beer at the bar I felt a relaxation as if a weight had been lifted from my shoulders. There was a wide distribution of ages and some of them appearing near to my own age. The bartender spoke good English and told me of other clubs in the area and one that many university students were known to go to. That amazed me thinking that if such a club had existed in Dundee when I went there how much my life would have been different. As the hours went by and the club filled up and loud music filled the air I realized that I could never have guessed that any of those men would be like me if I'd met them somewhere else. To be sure there were a few that I'd have guessed at but they were only a few. Most looked quite ordinary. We talked to a number of men there that night introduced to us by the bartender and Glenn would sometimes grin at me and say: "that one's interested in you," and I'd be pleased and tell him not to be so daft, they were only being friendly. I was impressed that many of them spoke English well. The night was a success and we returned to the student hotel merry and inebriated.

The following night we went back to the same club. By this time I was more comfortable and talked with people from other countries, tourists, enjoying the different accents, excited at the thought that Amsterdam wasn't far from England, a short flight from London, and I'd be able to go there even for a weekend after I had started work in Berkhamsted. It just happened that at one point two older Americans began to talk with us. I'd had several glasses of Heineken and challenged them. I knew there was another club upstairs that was taking in and getting legal help for American soldiers deserting from their army bases in Germany. I thought they'd come to the wrong club. I knew America was fighting a war in an Asian country called Vietnam. That confusion was soon cleared up as they explained they had already served their time in the armed forces and were veterans and lived in New York City and were visiting Amsterdam on holiday. Their names were Arthur and Michael and they had a flat in the city and worked on Wall Street and were ten years older than me. They talked of places in

138

Survivor

Greenwich Village in Manhattan, which was an area of streets with gay bars where men could live and go about their daily life and work in comfort. It didn't sound so unlikely to me then after walking the Leidsestraat and Leidseplein and going to that club, as though my eyes had become open and unclouded. We spent the next three days exploring Amsterdam with Arthur and Michael, talking of America and England and Scotland. Inevitably one day, as were having coffee outside a restaurant on the Damrak, I confessed to my feelings about the scars on my face. They laughed and teased me, Glenn joining in, saying that in America I would be seen as having 'rugged good looks' and I'd have no problems finding other lads interested in me. When I confessed more, saying I was looking for love they laughed even more and told me that's what everyone was looking for. They told me I should go to New York and find out. They wrote down their address and telephone number and I gave them my new address in Berkhamsted. I actually hadn't been there yet but it was all arranged. I was to be living in a boarding house c/o Mrs. Stossel, 41, Charles Street, Berkhamsted.

On the train back north to Edinburgh Glenn kept teasing me, smiling at me, telling me: "see...you are good looking...you've got rugged good looks." I'd flush and be pleased with him. We were friends for many years after that and he and his mother and aunt came to visit me in America after I settled in. He was the very best sort of friend anyone could have. We parted in Edinburgh Station, promising to keep in touch, and that we would meet again for my graduation, as he got the train to Glasgow and I got the train to Dundee. All I had to do there was pick up my large packed grey suitcase, the one I'd left Derby Street with, though now packed tight, and my bulky tape recorder. They had been stored in the luggage room of Belmont Hall. I left Dundee with a strange mix of sadness leaving a place I'd had so many good times, intermingled with hope for a better future ahead of me.

I had plenty of time to think and reflect on the train journey south from Edinburgh to Berkhamsted. It was almost four hundred miles and since I'd taken the train that stopped at local stations, not the Edinburgh to London express train, I had hours to look out the window and assess my past and potential future. I still had the

139

loneliness of not having a loving family, people who would understand what I had accomplished so far and would encourage me to do more. Josie had written me a warm and encouraging letter. My grandmother in Ballybohan had written congratulations. That was about it.

I've met good people in life and always tried to remember them, praying for them a couple of seconds as thought of them came to mind, just as the priests had taught me in St. Mary's College, sincere heartfelt thanks to God for them, meaning it, wanting their kindness to be known. I've met indifferent people who have puzzled me, wondering why they could not find pleasure in nature and weather and the sky and animals in the fields. Pessimism is alien to my nature and I cannot identify with it, nor wanted to. It was akin to me like putting wild animals in cages; a horrible thing. I've always looked for the silver lining in the darkest cloud. I've always believed that the woman who scrubs floors for a living and the man who breaks stones by the side of the road are my equal too. I've met bad people and they are the ones most difficult to detect, for often they are charming and manipulative. That is where family and brothers and sisters and cousins and uncles and aunts living close and nearby can look out and stand up and make warnings and alerts. That is when being lonely and alone is most dangerous. My only defense for such people was anger, trying to forget their name, working on forgetting where they lived.

Newcastle was the first stop. I looked out at the station, remembering the day I had fled north. Darlington was the next major stop, twelve miles west of Stockton-on-Tees. That brought thought of Patricia and Billy and how she was now safe, married to a man who loved her, who would do anything for her, who always held her hand walking down the street. To be sure she was still recovering from life in Derby Street but with Billy by her side. I hadn't known what had happened in the years I was in university. She had been tormented by our father after I left, turning his rages on her, attacking her like he had attacked me, deriding her, hurting her. Billy had grown stronger and had fought with him several times, bloody fights, injuries, protecting my sister. Patricia had gone to live with his parents. They had married October 1965, in St.

140

Mary's Church on Norton Road, buying the proper clothes for Tom and Terry to wear, going to live in a flat near Ropner Park. It wasn't far enough. Our father knew where she worked. It is a terrible thing for a father to call his daughter at work and threaten her, saying he'd stab her with a big knife if she didn't come back and bring her wage packet, continually demanding money, sending our pleading mother for money, threats of violence in Derby Street if she did not give, depleting the money she and Billy were saving for a deposit on a house. Mary and Tom and Terry were still there. Billy had surprised her after she had been driven to despair, in guilt that she had been tormented into giving some of their precious savings, that his frequent overtime bricklaying had been saved and was enough to put down a deposit to buy a house. He understood. He kept on holding her hand. He first bought them a house in town then later sold that and bought them a beautiful house several miles outside Stockton. Patricia loved it at first but then became lonely and feeling isolated away from his parents and her friends. She didn't tell Billy, not wanting him to be disappointed in her, until one night in bed she cried and told him. She fell asleep and awoke later in the night to hear hammering outside and looked out the bedroom window to see Billy putting a for sale sign on the front lawn, not waiting for the sun to come up, wanting it to be there when she awoke. Billy has always been there for my sister and it has been a joy to me.

York was next, the ancient Viking capital Jorvik, where Steve had come from, to work in I.C.I., a day release student like myself, and he being an upper class lad putting the idea into my working class head to dare to put down the University of St. Andrews as one of my choices on my university application form. I'm sure it was just a stray sentence to him. It had a major impact on my life and my future.

There were other stations before Berkhamsted but no reminisces and so my thoughts turned to Amsterdam and the thrilling idea that I might find love with someone who would think I had rugged good looks. The dream of finding my own Hephaestion was not dead. I could still imagine seeking out new

Survivor

knowledge, honor, integrity, heroic deeds with a companion by my side who would love me.

Mrs. Stossel was a good woman. She had five bedrooms she rented out to young men and women. She provided breakfast and dinner to those who wanted it. She reminded me of my grandmother in Ballybohan. I didn't get to know my fellow lodgers while I was there but I did get to know Mrs. Stossel and how she touched my heart telling me of the cruelty in the world. It began one evening as we had tea in her kitchen and she explained why she had such a house with so many bedrooms. She had been a young Jewish girl in Poland when the German army invaded on September 1, 1939. She had fled north with many hundreds of others, walking, hungry, in fear, amid warfare, in winter and snow, hiding in forests, finding good people and bad as they sought safety in Russia. As our evening conversations went by I felt identification with those poor suffering people and my dreams at night were filled with the agony that I had not been there to help them and protect them. I dreamed of my cousins who had never been born and the horror of the Great Hunger and Thomas Wade and the coffin ships. For as Mrs. Stossel continued I heard her tell me of walking when most of the adults died of hunger and wounds and despair, giving the children crusts of stale bread and moldy cheese as they gave up, dying in forests and ditches, urging their children to keep walking and not look back. Mrs. Stossel was a living witness to those things and I resolved to carry her stories forward in life; just as I carried the stories forward told me by my grandparents of hunger and disease and dying in fields and beside roads during the years of the Great Hunger. There were no coffin ships in Russia. The war was there too and few enough good people so they turned south and walked for over a year through warfare, hiding from soldiers, until they reached Istanbul and internment camps and food and clothes. Only she and about a dozen younger children had made it out of the many hundreds who fled away from almost inevitable concentration camps. After the war in Istanbul she met kind people from England who brought her and the younger children to Berkhamsted and gave them the house we sat in, the house where she adopted the children and raised them.

142

Survivor

Berkhamsted was a beautiful town, upscale as they say, with leafy trees shading the streets. The Research building was on the main street, a short walk from my lodging house. It was impressive from the outside and on walking into the laboratories. After I began work I soon became disappointed. The glassware was dusty and I had to scrounge for equipment. There was only one old infrared spectrometer shared by all the chemists. They didn't have a nuclear resonance spectrometer. The library was small. I didn't find the striving for excellence, the work ethic I had been trained in at I.C.I., the urge to do the very best job.

Within weeks I knew I didn't want to stay there. That placed me in a predicament. I didn't want to admit I'd made the wrong choice. It was a very good salary. I was going to make a lot of money. The rent with Mrs. Stossel was very reasonable. I was within a ten minute walk from work. But I wasn't happy with the job. It was not a challenge. I resolved to save as much money as I could. I began to look at Master of Science degrees at London University. I was interested in an M.S. degree program in Biochemistry. It was a full time one year program. I'd have to pay for it myself. I calculated I could easily save enough in one year to enroll, assuming that I could get a share in a student flat and the brochures I'd sent for indicated that was possible.

As the months went by I decided not to waste my money flying to Amsterdam. It was a temptation to me but I resisted. It was much more important to save my money to get into that Biochemistry program. I still had to return for the graduation ceremony at the University of St. Andrews. When that time came I took the train north and slept the night before in Glenn's room in Belmont Hall. He'd arranged for the rental of the gown I'd need for the ceremony and he had it in his room when I arrived.

Early the next morning we met up with his mother and his mother's sister at Dundee train station. They had got the train in from Glasgow to be there for me at the graduation. We then got the train for the town of St. Andrews in Fife. So it was on that day of October 11, 1967, I graduated from the University of St. Andrews in the town of St. Andrews, Scotland, the only Honours degree in Chemistry, the last such degree from Dundee while it was still part

143

of the University of St. Andrews. The print out schedule had my name, John Leonard Fahey, Roscommon, Eire (Chemistry). I'd done it. I had a document to send to my grandmother, to affirm my link with Ireland.

After the ceremony we returned to Dundee and had dinner at a good restaurant and I was so very happy I had them to share that day with me. After the dinner, in a pub near the train station, so we could have as much time as possible before I'd have to get a late train to Edinburgh, I shared with them a letter I'd received from Arthur in New York inviting me for a visit. He'd written that it was a holiday called Thanksgiving and there would be feasting and happiness and it would be with his extended family in another part of New York City called Brooklyn. It would be in the last week of November and I could stay with him in his flat in Elmhurst. Mrs. Taylor's sister told me I'd have to work fast because I'd need to apply for a visitor's visa at the American Embassy in London and the cheapest way to go would be on Icelandic Airlines. She knew of such things from her work in a real estate office. They all urged me to accept Arthur's offer, Glenn smiling and eyes twinkling in happiness for me. It was there I decided to do it, writing to Arthur on my return to Berkhamsted, asking if it would be alright for me to visit for two weeks, telephoning the American Embassy to ask on how to apply for a visitor's visa, applying at work to take my first year two weeks holiday early.

The Beatles had been to America several times while I had been in university and their album Sgt Pepper's Lonely Hearts Club Band had been the top of the charts since June. So much had changed in the world since I began university. So much hope, so much promise, and now I was going to cross the Atlantic. In an odd sort of coincidence a volcanic eruption off the south coast of Iceland had reached the surface in my first months of university and had continued to erupt, forming a new island, ending about the time I took my final examinations. Now I was flying through Iceland to America. It seemed like an omen, as though it was destiny.

I took the train from Berkhamsted to Glasgow. Mrs. Taylor met me there and went with me to the Airport. She was like a mother to me, fussing over me, telling me to have a good time,

144

Survivor

kissing me on the cheek as I readied myself to go to the embarkation line. I needed that and somehow she knew. I'd only flown between London and Amsterdam before. They were short flights. This flight was to be over an ocean. I made friends soon after I got on the plane with two American girls who were about my own age and had been on 'vacation' in Europe for several months. We had lots of fun and laughter as they educated me on the difference between American English and English spoken in England. I'd never thought of it before nor heard the quote that England and America were two countries separated by a common language. As we landed in Keflavik airport in Iceland to change planes for the flight to New York I'd realized it was a particularly apt quote. The airport was a new experience. There was a map in the airport informing us that we were one hundred and seventy seven miles south of the Arctic Circle. The hot water taps in the toilets informed us that the water came from hot springs. The airport was heated from hot springs. It was a different world, a volcanic country so far north.

On the way out from Iceland the pilots took us by Surtsey, the new volcanic island, banking the plane for a good look, then it was time for an excellent dinner and complimentary drinks. It was a large plane and almost fully occupied and it became warm and lots of conversations and American accents surrounded me. It was going to be a long flight and my new American friends advised me to settle in and try to get some sleep because of the 'time difference'. I couldn't. I didn't even know what they meant. I was too excited. As my companions fell asleep I wandered up and down the plane talking to many people, only taking a nap late at night, being awoken by a rise in the volume of conversations and talk of seeing Newfoundland. That thrilled me and though it was still many hours before we were to land at Kennedy Airport I constantly went back to the windows beside the kitchen area, looking out at the land passing beneath, daylight in the sky, in the company of others who could not sleep.

After landing I had to part ways from the two friendly American girls. They had an easier time, being American, and I had to join a long crowded line of visitors like myself. It took an

145

Survivor

astonishingly long time, edging forward, my new smaller suitcase bought for the holiday, at my feet. It was intimidating. I'd been told by other lodgers at Mrs. Stossel's boarding house that America was a military country and did I know it was at war. I'd told them the war was far from America. When I finally reached a counter with a man in a uniform, my heart was beating fast and I started to realize what was meant by the time difference. The man examined my passport and visitor's visa and the forms I'd filled out on the plane that had asked some peculiar questions. He asked me the purpose of my visit and other questions until I felt I was being interrogated. I had to put my suitcase on a table and another man searched it. They were not friendly until the end when the man who searched my suitcase wished me a good holiday and warned me to leave when my visa expired. I don't know why he said that. My return ticket was in his hand.

Arthur and Michael were waving at me amid the crowd on the far side of the metal barrier and I felt an exhausted sense of relief. I was impressed that Arthur had a Chevrolet car. I hadn't expected that. On the way to Elmhurst I fell asleep on the back seat and was only groggily awake as we had coffee in the kitchen of the flat, joking I now knew I should call it an apartment, that a flat was a puncture in a car tire. The coffee didn't keep me awake and I collapsed onto a bed and slept through until evening.

When I awoke I asked if I could take a bath. Arthur told me I could take a shower. I insisted that I wanted to take a bath. I'd never taken a shower, not sure it would get me clean, wanting to scrub myself and wash my hair. They laughed at that and told me to take my time at it and then we were going to out for pizza. I knew it was some kind of food. I hoped I would like it. I was very hungry.

When we came outside it was night and I saw we were in an area of four storey blocks of flats, correcting that in my mind to blocks of apartments, resolving to adjust to as much of these new words as I could while I was there. I noticed things. The signs for atomic bomb shelters troubled me. They told me that was from years ago. The papers blowing around on the street disturbed me. They told me that was good because it generated work for people

146

Survivor

who would otherwise be unemployed. It seemed somehow to be both very modern and Victorian to my eyes. It didn't seem as if I was in a huge city. The pizza shop was at the corner of the block. Arthur and Michael had clearly told the men behind the counter about me. I was given pizza and devoured it. It was extremely tasty. I had another and then another, slice by slice, standing at the counter, feeling a warm welcoming friendship around me. I was told to come down when Arthur and Michael were at work during the day and I'd get free pizza. That was my welcome to America, the America I'd learn to love.

That was enough for me for one night. I was still exhausted. They laughed and teased me, telling me I'd been hit by jet lag. I hadn't been in a jet. It was a turboprop. Apparently it was the same thing. It was a new experience. We went back to the apartment to watch American television and I fell asleep during it and slept all night long.

The next morning I woke early, totally refreshed, eager to go out into this new world. When Arthur and Michael got up it was my turn to tease them, calling them sleepyheads, telling them I was used to getting up early. It was the day of Thanksgiving and Arthur was to take me with him to Brooklyn. Michael was to go to his own family. So we had a light breakfast and I became engrossed watching American television, amazed there were so many channels, and in color. There was news of the war in Vietnam. It was serious. There were student demonstrations against the war. There was a military draft of young men. It gave me an uneasy feeling. Arthur told me not to talk of it. It wasn't the right day for it. It was a day to support the soldiers. I stopped asking questions about it. I didn't stop thinking about it.

My first Thanksgiving was a delight. I lost track of the names of the people I was introduced to. There was an enormous roast turkey. It was magnificent.

The next day Arthur took me into Manhattan and Wall Street and the Statue of Liberty. Late in the afternoon we met up with Michael in Greenwich Village and walked Christopher Street as they pointed out gay shops and businesses and bars. I was stunned. They told me most of the men passing us on the street were gay. I

147

Survivor

found that difficult to believe at first but when they took me into a bar called the Stonewall Inn I underwent a shivering understanding that what I'd been told was true. Most of them were quite ordinary people, even some of them looking tough enough to take on my father. When they asked me if I wanted to go dancing my evening took on an amazing texture. I was being asked to dance by other men, good looking men, men who thought I had rugged good looks. It all seemed to me to be very normal. It was going to take me a while to adjust to this new reality. It was as if I was on another planet. I had never imagined such a thing.

I suppose there are points in everyone's life that bring a sharp transition between the past and the future, a transition that must be negotiated with care, not plunged into with abandon and lack of caution. That was where I was glad I was with Arthur and Michael. They worked during the day and we went out to Greenwich Village at night. They told me that if someone came on to me I shouldn't go to his place, it could be dangerous; I should invite him back to their apartment. I thanked them and told them I was looking for love and it would be terrible to find it there when my visa was so limited. I had a job to go back to and plans to move to London to study for a graduate degree in Biochemistry. There was time enough for me. I could find love in Amsterdam, a short weekend flight from London, and I would be eternally grateful to them for letting me know I could be a real person, an honest person, equal to anyone else. They told me that they didn't go out every night usually. They were doing it because I was there. It wasn't like England where lots of men go out to the pub at night. That suited me fine. I wanted to spend more evenings watching American television. The world was a great deal more complicated than I had thought before.

I had the days to myself. I'd go down to the pizza shop for lunch and spend the day watching television and reading newspapers. One day I saw an advertisement for an Assistant Scientist in the New York Times. It was at the Warner-Lambert Research Institute in New Jersey. I looked at a map and saw it was about thirty miles west of New York City in a town called Morris Plains. I wanted so much to see if the research laboratories in

148

Survivor

America were like the ones in I.C.I. and that tugged at my curiosity. I knew it wasn't right for me to apply for a job I couldn't take but the hunger to see laboratories took over. I took down Arthur's typewriter from a shelf and wrote a letter of application and a description of my experience and degree. I put down Arthur's address and phone number. When he came home I showed him what I had typed and asked for a stamp and envelope, He was very helpful. He made some phone calls and found out that if I got an interview I could get a subway under the Hudson River to Hoboken on the other side and get a train from there to Morris Plains.

I got a phone call inviting me for an interview on a day three days before I was scheduled to return to England. I hadn't brought a suit with me but I had good trousers and a white shirt and tie. Arthur loaned me a jacket. I went with him to Wall Street on that day. He put me on an underground subway to Hoboken where I got the train to Morris Plains. I hadn't yet adjusted to American money but the people in the station were helpful. It was only an hour on the train and then I was walking a mile up a nice country road seeing the Warner-Lambert buildings ahead of me. As I walked up the drive to the entrance lobby it felt just right to me. The two storey brick buildings were set in tidy lawns and a large car park was filled with cars to one side. I didn't have to wait very long until Dr. Wittekind, the scientist looking for an assistant, came to get me. I had a wonderful day being taken around the laboratories. They were everything I wished I could have found in Berkhamsted. They had an infrared spectrometer for each two laboratories. There was a woman in each laboratory to clean glassware. There was a modern nuclear resonance spectrometer run by a handsome young man in a wheelchair. They had their own structure analysis laboratory run by a woman called Unni Zeek, an immigrant scientist from Norway. I met Dr. Maximilian von Strondtman, an immigrant from Kiev in the Ukraine, who seemed to take a liking to me, insisting that he be included in the lunch. I didn't know they were going to be taking me to lunch. It seemed as if there were many foreign scientists there. I wished so much I could have found such a job in England, overwhelmed that they were being so considerate to me and I was going to have to tell them that I was going back to England.

149

Survivor

We were joined at lunch by Dr. John Shavel, the head of the department. I found myself being drawn into telling him about my work with Dr. Watson and enthusiasm gripped me, writing structures of the optically active dihydrotetrazine and tetrazine and that Dr. Watson had sent them to the University of London for Circular Dichroism and Optical Rotary Dispersion studies. I wished so much that I'd found them in England and confessed I was only on a visitor's visa and was going back to England in three days. Dr. Shavel took me back to his office and sat looking at me with a quizzical look on his face. I apologized for wasting his time. His response was totally unexpected. He asked me what it was like going to night school at Stockton-Billingham Technical College. He asked me about my work in I.C.I. and the Standardisation Laboratory. He asked why I had not gone on to do a doctorate after graduating from St. Andrews University. I explained to him that I'd only got a third class Honours degree and that wasn't good enough to be accepted into a doctoral program. He raised his eyebrows at that and commented he knew that a Ph.D. program in British university could only be done full time.

I told him I still had plans. I was going to save my money and apply to do a masters degree in Biochemistry at London University. He smiled at me and told me I could do a Ph.D. part time with evening classes at a university in Hoboken, Stevens Institute of Technology, and since I was already used to night classes and after all an Honours degree was an Honours degree and Warner-Lambert would pay my tuition.

I was reluctant to believe him. I pointed out again that in three days I had to leave. I only had a visitor's visa. He told me the company lawyer could get me what he called a green card; a legal authorization to live and work in America. I was weakening. I surrendered when he wrote down a number on a piece of paper and pushed it across the table at me. I looked down and exchange rate calculations rapidly ran through my head. It was more than three times than my salary in Berkhamsted. I accepted, surprised at myself for my quick decision, hoping I was doing the right thing.

I had a great deal to do. When I told Arthur and Michael they promised to help me, telling me I'd have to learn how to drive a car

150

and then buy a car. Dr. Shavel had told me I could get an apartment within walking distance of the laboratories. He'd said flat at first and grinned when I was startled. He told me they'd send me a letter to Berkhamsted when it was time to go to the American Embassy to get my interview and green card. He told me to get a direct TWA flight back to New York. The company would reimburse me. I was to report to the personnel office when I started work and I'd be given one month's money for the cost of a local motel while I settled in.

I returned to Berkhamsted for my final months of work, packed all of my belongings and tape recorder into a trunk, getting it ready to ship it by sea to Arthur's address, started packing my old grey suitcase, wrote letters, went through weeks of bewilderment at the change in my fortunes, preparing myself for a new life, and wondering, wondering all the time if I was making the right decision.

It was the right decision. I flew to America February 13, 1968. I did get my Ph.D. and began a career of scientific accomplishment. My scars did get smoothed out, my tremors were diagnosed as benign, and I did find love.

THE END

Printed in Poland
by Amazon Fulfillment
Poland Sp. z o.o., Wrocław